AF004746

How to access your on-line resources

Kaplan Financial students will have a MyKaplan account and these extra resources will be available to you online. You do not need to register again, as this process was completed when you enrolled. If you are having problems accessing online materials, please ask your course administrator.

If you are not studying with Kaplan and did not purchase your book via a Kaplan website, to unlock your extra online resources please go to **www.en-gage.co.uk** (even if you have set up an account and registered books previously). You will then need to enter the ISBN number (on the title page and back cover) and the unique pass key number contained in the scratch panel below to gain access.

You will also be required to enter additional information during this process to set up or confirm your account details.

If you purchased through the Kaplan Publishing website you will automatically receive an e-mail invitation to register your details and gain access to your content. If you do not receive the e-mail or book content, please contact Kaplan Publishing.

This code can only be used once for the registration of this book online. This registration and your online content will expire when the examinations covered by this book have taken place. Please allow one hour from the time you submit your book details for us to process your request.

Please scratch the film to access your unique code.

Please be aware that this code is case-sensitive and you will need to include the dashes within the passcode, but not when entering the ISBN.

CIMA's CGMA 2019 Professional Examinations

CIMA's CGMA Strategic Level

Subject E3

Strategic Management

EXAM PRACTICE KIT

SUBJECT E3 : STRATEGIC MANAGEMENT

British Library Cataloguing-in-Publication Data

A catalogue record for this book is available from the British Library.

Published by:

Kaplan Publishing UK
Unit 2 The Business Centre
Molly Millar's Lane
Wokingham
Berkshire
RG41 2QZ

ISBN: 978-1-83996-476-3

© Kaplan Financial Limited, 2023

No part of this publication may be reproduced, stored in a retrieval system or transmitted in any form or by any means electronic, mechanical, photocopying, recording or otherwise without the prior written permission of the publisher.

The text in this material and any others made available by any Kaplan Group company does not amount to advice on a particular matter and should not be taken as such. No reliance should be placed on the content as the basis for any investment or other decision or in connection with any advice given to third parties. Please consult your appropriate professional adviser as necessary. Kaplan Publishing Limited, all other Kaplan group companies, the International Accounting Standards Board, and the IFRS Foundation expressly disclaim all liability to any person in respect of any losses or other claims, whether direct, indirect, incidental, consequential or otherwise arising in relation to the use of such materials. Printed and bound in Great Britain.

Kaplan Publishing's learning materials are designed to help students succeed in their examinations. In certain circumstances, CIMA® can make post-exam adjustment to a student's mark or grade to reflect adverse circumstances which may have disadvantaged a student's ability to take an exam or demonstrate their normal level of attainment (see CIMA's Special Consideration policy). However, it should be noted that students will not be eligible for special consideration by CIMA if preparation for or performance in a CIMA exam is affected by any failure by their tuition provider to prepare them properly for the exam for any reason including, but not limited to, staff shortages, building work or a lack of facilities etc.

Similarly, CIMA will not accept applications for special consideration on any of the following grounds:

- failure by a tuition provider to cover the whole syllabus

- failure by the student to cover the whole syllabus, for instance as a result of joining a course part way through

- failure by the student to prepare adequately for the exam, or to use the correct pre-seen material

- errors in the Kaplan Official Study Text, including sample (practice) questions or any other Kaplan content or

- errors in any other study materials (from any other tuition provider or publisher).

CONTENTS

	Page
Index to questions and answers	P.5
Exam techniques	P.7
Syllabus guidance, learning objectives and verbs	P.9
Approach to revision	P.13
Syllabus grids	P.15

Section

1	Objective test questions	1
2	Answers to objective test questions	77

Quality and accuracy are of the utmost importance to us so if you spot an error in any of our products, please send an email to mykaplanreporting@kaplan.com with full details.

Our Quality Co-ordinator will work with our technical team to verify the error and take action to ensure it is corrected in future editions.

SUBJECT E3 : STRATEGIC MANAGEMENT

INDEX TO QUESTIONS AND ANSWERS

OBJECTIVE TEST QUESTIONS

	Page number	
	Question	Answer
The strategy process – 15%	**1**	**77**
The process of strategy formulation	1	77
Mission, vision, values and stakeholders	5	79
Governance, ethics, and corporate social responsibility	10	81
Analysing the organisational ecosystem – 20%	**14**	**83**
External environmental analysis	14	83
Strategic networks and platforms	23	86
Resources and value creation within the organisational ecosystem	27	88
Generating strategic options – 15%	**35**	**91**
Framework for generating strategic options	35	91
Strategic options	38	93
Making strategic choices – 15%	**43**	**95**
Portfolio analysis	43	95
Strategy evaluation	45	96
Strategic control – 20%	**48**	**97**
Performance management systems	48	97
Change management	54	101
Digital strategy – 15%	**66**	**106**
Digital technologies	66	106
Elements of digital strategy	70	107

EXAM TECHNIQUES

COMPUTER-BASED ASSESSMENT

Golden rules

1   Make sure you have completed the compulsory 15-minute tutorial before you start the test. This tutorial is available through the AICPA & CIMA website and focusses on the functionality of the exam. You cannot speak to the invigilator once you have started.

2   These exam practice kits give you plenty of exam style questions to practise so make sure you use them to fully prepare.

3   Attempt all questions, there is no negative marking.

4   Double check your answer before you put in the final answer although you can change your response as many times as you like.

5   Not all questions will be multiple choice questions (MCQs) – you may have to fill in missing words or figures.

6   Identify the easy questions first and get some points on the board to build up your confidence.

7   Attempt 'wordy' questions first as these may be quicker than the computation style questions. This will relieve some of the time pressure you will be under during the exam.

8   If you don't know the answer, flag the question and attempt it later. In your final review before the end of the exam try a process of elimination.

9   Work out your answer on the whiteboard provided first if it is easier for you. There is also an onscreen 'scratch pad' on which you can make notes. You are not allowed to take pens, pencils, rulers, pencil cases, phones, paper or notes into the testing room.

SYLLABUS GUIDANCE, LEARNING OBJECTIVES AND VERBS

A   CIMA's CGMA® 2019 PROFESSIONAL QUALIFICATION

Details regarding the content of the CIMA's CGMA 2019 Professional Qualification can be located within the CGMA 2019 Professional Qualification syllabus document.

You can use the following diagram showing the whole structure of your qualification to help you keep track of your progress. Make sure you seek appropriate advice if you are unsure about your progression through the qualification.

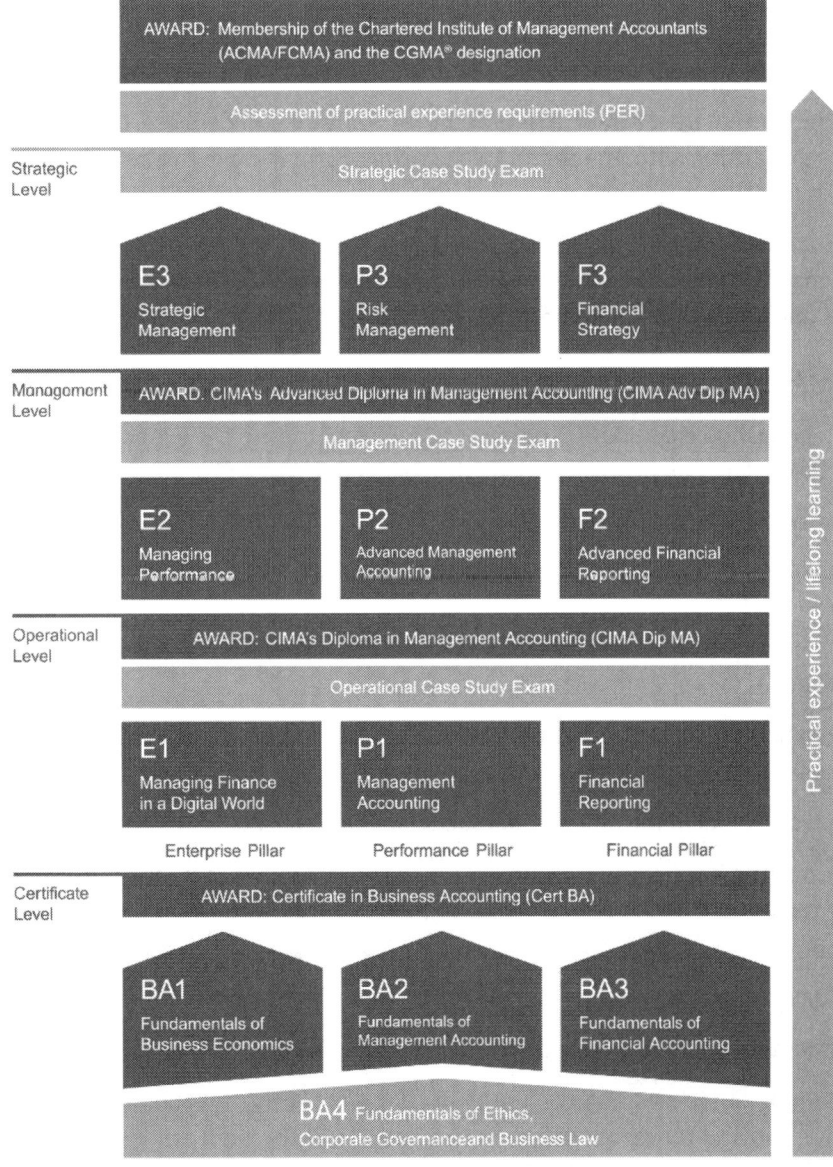

Reproduced with CIMA's permission

SUBJECT E3 : STRATEGIC MANAGEMENT

B STUDY WEIGHTINGS

A percentage weighting is shown against each exam content area in CIMA's CGMA® Exam Blueprints. This is intended as a guide to the proportion of study time each topic requires.

All component learning outcomes will be tested.

The weightings do not specify the number of marks that will be allocated to topics in the examination.

C LEARNING OUTCOMES

Each subject within the qualification is divided into a number of broad syllabus topics. The topics contain one or more lead learning outcomes, related component learning outcomes and indicative knowledge content.

A learning outcome has two main purposes:

1. to define the skill or ability that a well-prepared candidate should be able to exhibit in the examination
2. to demonstrate the approach likely to be taken by examiners in examination questions.

The learning outcomes are part of a hierarchy of learning objectives. The verbs used at the beginning of each learning outcome relate to a specific learning objective, e.g. Evaluate alternative approaches to budgeting.

The verb 'evaluate' indicates a high-level learning objective. As learning objectives are hierarchical, it is expected that at this level students will have knowledge of different budgeting systems and methodologies and be able to apply them.

CIMA's CGMA Exam Blueprints and representative task statements

CIMA have also published examination blueprints giving learners clear expectations regarding what is expected of them. This can be accessed via the AICPA & CIMA website.

The blueprint is structured as follows:

- Exam content sections (reflecting the syllabus document)
- Lead and component outcomes (reflecting the syllabus document)
- Representative task statements.

A representative task statement is a plain English description of what a CGMA® qualified finance professional should know and be able to do.

The content and skill level determine the language and verbs used in the representative task.

CIMA will test up to the level of the task statement in the Objective Test (an Objective Test question on a particular topic could be set at a lower level than the task statement in the blueprint).

The format of the Objective Test blueprints follows that of the published syllabus for the 2019 Professional Qualification.

Weightings for content sections are also included in the individual subject blueprints.

A list of the learning objectives and the verbs that appear in the syllabus learning outcomes and examinations follows and these will help you to understand the depth and breadth required for a topic and the skill level the topic relates to.

CIMA's verb hierarchy

Skill level	Verbs used	Definition
Level 5 **Evaluation** How you are expected to use your learning to evaluate, make decisions or recommendations	Advise	Counsel, inform or notify
	Assess	Evaluate or estimate the nature, ability or quality of
	Evaluate	Appraise or assess the value of
	Recommend	Propose a course of action
	Review	Assess and evaluate in order, to change if necessary
Level 4 **Analysis** How you are expected to analyse the detail of what you have learned	Align	Arrange in an orderly way
	Analyse	Examine in detail the structure of
	Communicate	Share or exchange information
	Compare and contrast	Show the similarities and/or differences between
	Develop	Grow and expand a concept
	Discuss	Examine in detail by argument
	Examine	Inspect thoroughly
	Interpret	Translate into intelligible or familiar terms
	Monitor	Observe and check the progress of
	Prioritise	Place in order of priority or sequence for action
	Produce	Create or bring into existence
Level 3 **Application** How you are expected to apply your knowledge	Apply	Put to practical use
	Calculate	Ascertain or reckon mathematically
	Conduct	Organise and carry out
	Demonstrate	Prove with certainty or exhibit by practical means
	Prepare	Make or get ready for use
	Reconcile	Make or prove consistent/compatible
Level 2 **Comprehension** What you are expected to understand	Describe	Communicate the key features of
	Distinguish	Highlight the differences between
	Explain	Make clear or intelligible/state the meaning or purpose of
	Identify	Recognise, establish or select after consideration
	Illustrate	Use an example to describe or explain something
Level 1 **Knowledge** What you are expected to know	List	Make a list of
	State	Express, fully or clearly, the details/facts of
	Define	Give the exact meaning of
	Outline	Give a summary of

D OBJECTIVE TEST

Objective Test

Objective Test questions require you to choose or provide a response to a question whose correct answer is predetermined.

The most common types of Objective Test question you will see are:

- Multiple choice, where you have to choose the correct answer(s) from a list of possible answers. This could either be numbers or text.
- Multiple response, for example, choosing two correct answers from a list of eight possible answers. This could either be numbers or text.
- Fill in the blank, where you fill in your answer within the provided space.
- Drag and drop, for example, matching a technical term with the correct definition.
- Hot spots, where you select an answer by clicking on graphs/diagrams.

Guidance re CIMA's on-screen calculator

As part of the CGMA Objective Test software, candidates are now provided with a calculator. This calculator is on-screen and is available for the duration of the assessment. The calculator is available in each of the objective tests and is accessed by clicking the calculator button in the top left hand corner of the screen at any time during the assessment. Candidates are permitted to utilise personal calculators as long as they are an approved CIMA model. CIMA approved model list can be found on the AICPA & CIMA website.

All candidates must complete a 15-minute exam tutorial before the assessment begins and will have the opportunity to familiarise themselves with the calculator and practise using it. The exam tutorial is also available online via the AICPA & CIMA website. Candidates can use their own calculators providing it is included in CIMA's authorised calculator listing.

Fundamentals of Objective Tests

The Objective Tests are 90-minute assessments comprising 60 compulsory questions, with one or more parts. There will be no choice and all questions should be attempted. All elements of a question must be answered correctly for the question to be marked correctly. All questions are equally weighted.

APPROACH TO REVISION

Stage 1: Assess areas of strengths and weaknesses

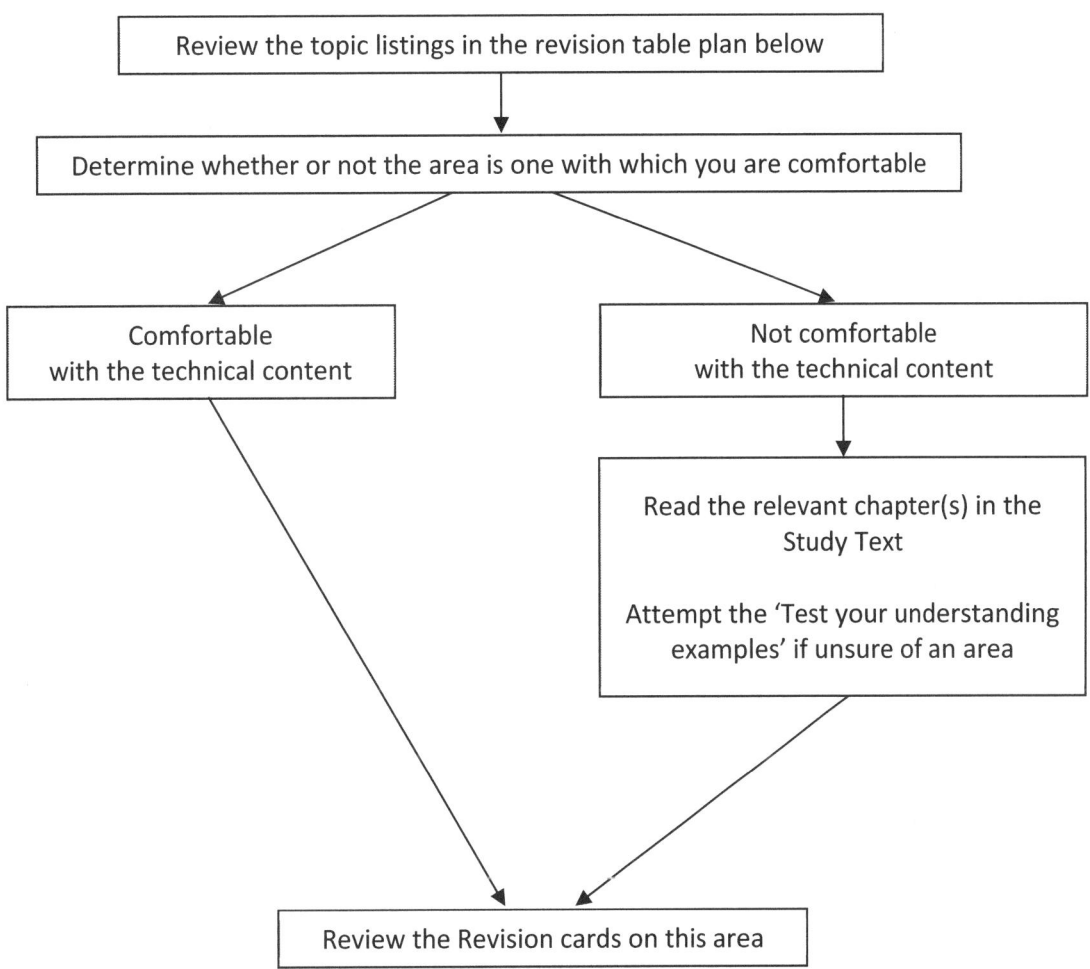

Stage 2: Question practice

Follow the order of revision of topics as recommended in the revision table plan below and attempt the questions in the order suggested.

Try to avoid referring to text books and notes and the model answer until you have completed your attempt.

Try to answer the question in the allotted time.

Review your attempt with the model answer and assess how much of the answer you achieved in the allocated exam time.

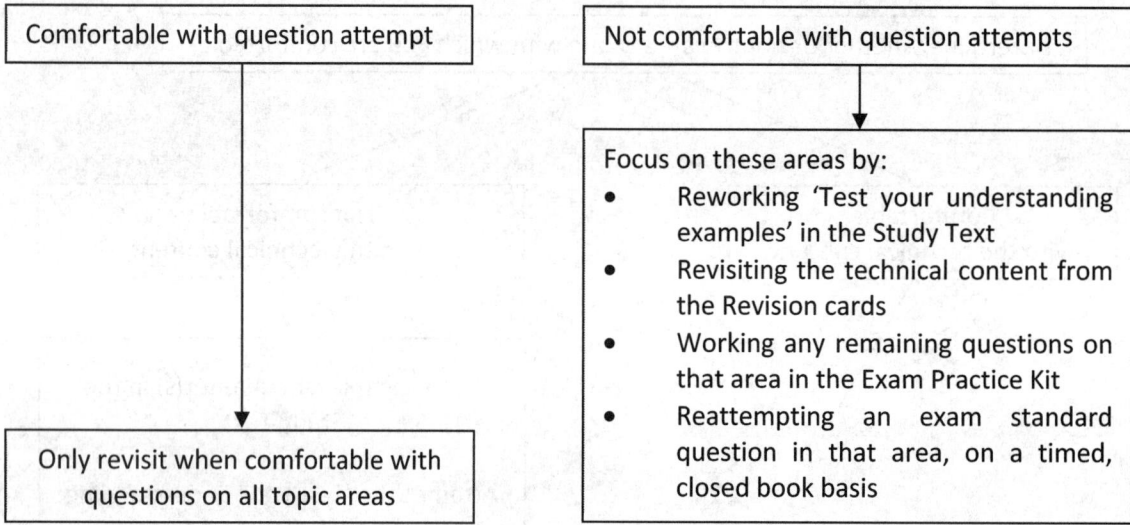

Stage 3: Final pre-exam revision

We recommend that you **attempt at least one ninety minute mock examination** containing a set of previously unseen exam standard questions.

It is important that you get a feel for the breadth of coverage of a real exam without advanced knowledge of the topic areas covered – just as you will expect to see on the real exam day.

Ideally a mock examination offered by your tuition provider should be sat in timed, closed book, real exam conditions.

CGMA SYLLABUS GRIDS

E3: Strategic Management

Formulate strategy and create conditions for successful implementation

Content weighting

Content area		Weighting
A	The strategy process	15%
B	Analysing the organisational ecosystem	20%
C	Generating strategic options	15%
D	Making strategic choices	15%
E	Strategic control	20%
F	Digital strategy	15%
		100%

SUBJECT E3 : STRATEGIC MANAGEMENT

E3A: The strategy process

Strategy is at the heart of what organisations do. This section provides the foundation of strategic management for the organisation. It introduces the strategy process that is elaborated on in the rest of the subject.

Lead outcome	Component outcome	Topics to be covered	Explanatory notes
1. Explain the purpose of strategy.	a. Define strategy. b. Explain the purpose of strategy.	• Different definitions of strategy • Essential features and characteristics of strategy	This section introduces the rest of E3. It provides the various definitions of strategy and outlines its essential features and characteristics. It discusses the different types and levels of strategy and the leaders who have responsibility for them. Finally, it looks at the strategy process from both the rational and emergent perspectives.
2. Discuss the types and levels strategy.	Discuss a. Types of strategy b. Levels of strategy	• Intended and emergent strategy • Corporate, business and functional strategies	
3. Outline the strategy process.	a. Outline the rational and emergent processes of arriving at strategy.	• Analysis of organisational ecosystem • Generating options • Strategic choice • Strategic control	

E3B: Analysing the organisational ecosystem

Every organisation inhabits an ecosystem within which it adapts and evolves. This ecosystem comprises markets and society, has its players and its own system of governance. Organisations can also join with others to form a smaller ecosystem within the broader one to reflect their strategic preferences. This section provides candidates with an understanding of the dynamics of the ecosystem (both the wider and the smaller more deliberate ones formed by organisations) and how it affects the strategy of the organisation.

Lead outcome	Component outcome	Topics to be covered	Explanatory notes
1. Analyse the elements of the ecosystem.	Analyse a. Markets and competition b. Society and regulation	• SWOT analysis • PESTEL analysis • Competitor analysis • Customer analysis • Wider ecosystems • Industry ecosystems	What types of markets do organisations operate in? What are the 'rules of the game' in these markets? What are the sources and opportunities for disruption in the market? How does society regulate the markets and provide 'permission to play' for organisations?
2. Discuss drivers of change in the ecosystem.	Discuss the following drivers of change: a. Institutional and systemic b. Social c. Market d. Technology e. Sustainability	• Globalisation • Geopolitics • Demography • Customer empowerment • Digital technology • Automation	What are the drivers of change in the ecosystem? How are the individual drivers linked? What type of outcomes do they bring individually and collectively? What risks and opportunities do they bring organisations?
3. Discuss the impact of the ecosystem on organisational strategy.	a. Discuss the impact of strategic networks and platforms on organisational strategy b. Conduct stakeholder analysis in networks	• Value creation in ecosystems • Participants and interactions in networks and platforms • Technology enablers in networks • Process of creating networks and platforms • Stakeholder analysis in networks • Corporate social responsibility	In a digital world what is the importance of networks and platforms? What are the roles, interactions, and governance systems in the ecosystems? Who are the key players? How does this affect the business model of organisations?

E3C: Generating strategic options

Strategy is about choice of options. These options must be generated and developed based on the dynamics of the ecosystem in which the organisation operates and the foundational contexts of the organisation (e.g. its purpose, values etc). This section covers how options are generated and links them to the purpose, values and vision of the organisation. In addition, it looks at the role of various parts and levels of the organisation in the strategy process.

Lead outcome	Component outcome	Topics to be covered	Explanatory notes
1. Discuss the context of generating options.	Discuss: a. The role of governance and ethics in the strategy process b. The purpose, vision and values of the organisation and their impact on strategy	• Roles and responsibility of leaders of organisations for strategy • Definition of purpose, vision and values of organisations • Linkage between purpose, vision and values to each other and to strategy	Who is responsible for various aspects of the strategy formulation process? How are those roles determined and governed? How does the organisation derive its purpose, vision and values? What processes exist to ensure that strategy is based on and/or are aligned to these?
2. Discuss how to generate and develop options.	Discuss how to: a. Frame key strategic questions b. Diagnose organisation's starting position c. Forecast potential organisational operating ecosystem d. Use various frameworks to generate options	• Product/market matrix • Generic strategies • Trend analysis • System modelling • Scenario planning • Tangible and intangible value drivers and data to measure them • Game theory perspectives • Real option perspectives	What are the core strategic questions to ask and what are the criteria and constraints for asking them? What is the organisation's starting point? Where and how does it make money? What potential futures might it inhabit and what are the forces potentially driving these futures? What are the potential pathways to this future? What new business models are in play?

E3D: Making strategic choices

Once options have been generated in various areas of the organisation's operations the organisation has to choose between the alternatives. The choice is based on predefined criteria and an evaluation of the options against these criteria. The various options chosen must then be integrated into a coherent whole to form the organisation's strategy. This section covers how the options are evaluated, chosen and integrated coherently to form the strategy of the organisation.

Lead outcome	Component outcome	Topics to be covered	Explanatory notes
1. Evaluate options.	a. Develop criteria for evaluation. b. Evaluate options against criteria. c. Recommend appropriate options.	• Suitability, acceptability and feasibility framework	What are the different criteria to guide the choice of options, one how are they prioritised and why?
2. Produce strategy by the integration of choices into coherent strategy.	Conduct: a. Value analysis b. Portfolio analysis	• Value chain analysis • Managing product portfolio	What are the criteria to ensure effective integration and why? What are the trade-offs to be made when putting the individual choices together? How does one ensure integrated thinking?

SUBJECT E3 : STRATEGIC MANAGEMENT

E3E: Strategic control

Once strategy has been formulated, it has to be implemented. This involves developing and communicating action plans, allocating resources and monitoring the implementation of the plans. In addition, implementing strategy involves significant change. The nature of these changes should be evaluated and appropriate ways of managing change have to be developed and implemented. This section examines how these implementation objectives are achieved and how change is managed.

Lead outcome	Component outcome	Topics to be covered	Explanatory notes
1. Develop strategic performance management system.	a. Develop detailed action plans b. Communicate action plans c. Monitor implementation d. Align incentives to performance	• Action plans • Target setting • Critical success factors (CSFs) • Key performance indicators (KPIs)	How does the organisation prepare the grounds for executing strategy? How does it create and communicate action plans for implementation? How is the whole organisation mobilised, motivated and incentivised to implement the plans? What role can integrated reporting play?
2. Advise on resource allocation to support strategy implementation.	a. Advise on resource availability b. Align resource allocation to strategic choices	• Audit of key resources and capabilities required to implement strategy • Matching resources to strategy	What are the resources needed to implement strategy? Where are the resources needed? How does the organisation re-align resource allocation from existing units or projects to new ones that match the strategic choices made?
3. Recommend change management techniques and methodologies.	a. Assess impact of strategy on organisation b. Recommend change management strategies c. Discuss the role of the leader in managing change	• Types of change • Impact of change on organisational culture • Resistance to change • Approaches and styles of change management • Role of change leader in communication	What is the impact of the new strategy on the whole organisation, parts of the organisation and partners of the organisation? What transformation is required and how does the organisation drive these changes?

E3F: Digital strategy

Strategy takes place within specific organisational contexts and ecosystems. The primary characteristics of the current context is digital transformation. Organisations need to think through their approach to strategy within this perspective. This section covers how to introduce thinking about digital transformation in the strategy of organisations.

Lead outcome	Component outcome	Topics to be covered	Explanatory notes
1. Describe the governance of digital transformation.	a. Describe the roles and responsibilities of the board and executive leadership in digital strategy.	• Role of board and senior leadership in digital strategy	Who is responsible for leading the process of digital transformation? What is their role in the process and why?
2. Analyse digital transformation.	Analyse a. Digital technologies b. Digital enterprise	• Cloud computing • Big data analytics • Process automation • Artificial intelligence • Data visualisation • Blockchain • Internet of things • Mobile • 3-D printing	What are the technologies that underpin digital transformation? How are they evolving and what impact do they have on the organisation and its immediate and wider operating environment? What type of organisation do such technologies create? What are the elements of the business and operating models of such digital enterprises.
3. Discuss the various elements of digital strategies.	Discuss: a. Economics of digitisation b. Digital ecosystems c. Digital consumption d. Data and metrics e. Leadership and culture	• Business case for digital transformation • Participants, interactions and dynamics of ecosystem and impact on strategy • Trends in consumption (e.g., hyper personalisation, move from products and services to experience) • New metrics (scale, active usage and engagement metrics) • Leadership in digital transformation	What is the economic and business case for digitisation? How does the organisation create partnerships in the ecosystem to ensure strategic success? What are key trends underlying the consumption of the organisation's products and services by customers and consumers? What data and metrics should organisations use to evaluate success of digital enterprises? How should leaders and their organisations think, act and react differently because of digital transformation?

SUBJECT E3 : STRATEGIC MANAGEMENT

Information concerning formulae and tables will be provided via the CIMA website, www.aicpa-cima.com

Section 1

OBJECTIVE TEST QUESTIONS

THE STRATEGY PROCESS – 15%

THE PROCESS OF STRATEGY FORMULATION

1	Q plc currently sells its product in two major markets – Europe and Asia. While it is a market leader in Europe, Q has struggled to penetrate the more competitive Asian market. It has therefore decided to pull out of Asia entirely and focus on its European markets.

Which ONE of the following levels of strategy does Q's decision relate to?

	A	Business
	B	Functional
	C	Operational
	D	Corporate

2	HY Ltd manufactures lamps in country L.

Which ONE of the following is consistent with an operational level strategy?

	A	Decision to launch a new range of novelty light bulbs
	B	Expansion into selling all HY goods in country F
	C	Creation of a new marketing campaign for HY's range of table lamps
	D	Decision to reduce floor lamp prices to match a competitor

SUBJECT E3 : STRATEGIC MANAGEMENT

3 X is a small conglomerate, consisting of a holding company based at a head office in the capital city of the country and five subsidiaries, each based in a different city. The subsidiaries operate in different industries, but X believes that it adds value by providing excellent top level management and consistent support systems.

X has recently acquired E, a manufacturing company. The CEO of X has arranged a meeting with the Board of E to discuss E's generic strategy, as the CEO believes that a change from cost leadership to differentiation would be appropriate. The Operations Director of E is also attending the meeting, to explain to the Board of E how the Management Information System of X Group is to be introduced to E.

Analyse the information provided about X, and categorise the following elements of strategy:

The decision, by X, to acquire E, is an example of _____1_____ strategy.

The implementation of common information systems, throughout the X group, is an example of _____2_____ strategy.

The decision whether to pursue cost leadership or differentiation within E is an example of _____3_____ strategy.

Use the terms below to fill in the missing words in gaps 1 and 2.

Note that each term can be used more than once.

- A Business
- B Functional
- C Corporate

4 AHQ has recently decided to install a new IT system to improve the efficiency of its payroll function. AHQ believes this will reduce the cost of running the payroll system by 15%.

Which ONE of the following levels of strategy is the above IT system most closely linked to?

- A Functional
- B Corporate
- C Business
- D Strategic

5 One of the problems with formal planning processes is that an organisation's analysis of its position is likely to be incomplete, leading to ineffective strategies being selected. This issue is known as _____.

Which ONE of the following two-word terms fills the gap in the sentence above?

- A Bounded rationality
- B Operational inefficiency
- C Rational model
- D Management distrust

OBJECTIVE TEST QUESTIONS : SECTION 1

6 C has just started a dog grooming business. She has no experience of this industry, but identified it as having potential for significant future growth. The market is relatively stable, with few innovations or changes occurring each year.

As C has invested a significant proportion of her life savings into the business, she wishes to consider her approach to creating an initial business strategy. She has some experience of strategic development and has a large amount of spare time to devote to her new business.

Which ONE of the following strategic planning models would be most suitable for C's business?

- A Emergent
- B Incrementalism
- C Rational Model
- D Freewheeling

7 **Which TWO of the following statements are consistent with a freewheeling opportunistic approach to strategy development?**

- A Good for fast-moving industries
- B Involves the adaptation of formal strategies for unexpected events
- C Good for inexperienced managers
- D Strategy tends to be small-scale changes to successful past policies
- E May make it difficult to raise external finance

8 X is a public utility, generating and distributing electricity. Until last year, X was publicly owned. X was then privatised, and is now owned by a range of institutional investors, and a large number of private individuals.

When X was owned by the State, it was provided each year with a list of assumptions to be used as a basis for strategic planning. Those assumptions each related to a variable in the planning process, such as 'assume price increases of 2%', or 'assume customer numbers increase by 1.3%'. The mission of X was 'to provide continuity of electricity supply, at affordable prices'.

X now has to start formally planning for long term shareholder value.

Categorise the previous planning approach of X, and recommend a more suitable alternative approach.

X previously took _____1_____ approach to its strategic planning. In order to achieve its aims, X should adopt _____2_____ approach.

Use the options below to fill in the missing words in gaps 1 and 2.

- A an emergent
- B a rational
- C an incremental

SUBJECT E3 : STRATEGIC MANAGEMENT

9 YU is a charity based in country K which aims to offer value for money. It has been set up to manage an area of woodland on behalf of the local population. YU aims to have around 3,000 visitors to the woodland every year, but in the last year it has only had around half of this number. YU has spent the same amount on advertising as in previous years, but has moved from using leaflets to radio advertisements. While YU was able to buy a large amount of radio advertising, YU's directors were unaware that the chosen station had relatively low numbers of listeners.

With reference to value for money, the low number of visitors indicates that YU has failed with regards to ____1____ over the past year. Its poor use of its advertising budget also indicates a lack of ____2____.

Use the options below to fill in the missing words in gaps 1 and 2.

Note that each term can be used more than once.

- A   Effectiveness
- B   Economy
- C   Ethics
- D   Efficiency
- E   Expertise

10 The following four companies have taken varying approaches to strategic planning. Which of the companies have/has adopted a traditional approach? (Select ALL that apply).

- A   Company J has identified that its shareholders want to see a 5% increase in dividends in the coming year.
- B   Company X has a strong relationship with its staff. It wishes to use this to increase the amount of work each staff member undertakes, enabling significant cost savings to be made.
- C   Company Q's major customer accounts for around 45% of Q's sales. They have recently told Q that they wish to see significant changes to Q's product. Q has not discussed this with their other customers, but has begun considering how to implement the requested changes.
- D   Company P has undertaken a detailed analysis of customer needs and competitor prices in its market. It has decided that it needs to reduce selling prices significantly to make itself more competitive.

11 Which THREE of the following are among the duties of a company director in the UK, as codified by the Companies Act 2006?

- A   the duty to act with consideration for all stakeholders
- B   the duty to act within powers
- C   the duty to exercise independent judgement
- D   the duty to follow all relevant ethical codes
- E   the duty not to accept benefits from third parties

12 HMN plc is a UK-based company. It is aware that all of its directors are currently from similar ethnic and educational backgrounds.

Good corporate governance suggests that companies like HMN should have a mix of directors with differing experiences and backgrounds. Which ONE strategic benefit is this likely to have to the company?

  A   Increased disclosure to stakeholders in general

  B   Increased ability to make sound strategic decisions

  C   Increased likelihood of the organisation being run on ethical grounds

  D   Increased transparency of the organisation

13 Consider the following statements:

  (i)   Strategic management accountants tend to focus on internal and external factors in their analysis.

  (ii) Traditional management accountants typically focused on historic business performance, while strategic management accountants need to be more forward-looking.

  Which of these statements is/are correct?

  A   (i) only

  B   (ii) only

  C   Both

  D   Neither

MISSION, VISION, VALUES AND STAKEHOLDERS

14 Y has recently published the following statement:

  'Y aims to continually improve shareholder value, by providing the best customer service in the industry to customers.'

  Which ONE of the following is this statement most likely to be?

  A   An objective

  B   A vision statement

  C   A non-market strategy statement

  D   A mission statement

15 **Which TWO of the following statements regarding an organisation's mission statements are correct?**

  A   They set out the long-term aspirations of the organisation

  B   They can be used to help create a desired corporate culture

  C   They are confidential and only meant to be circulated within the organisation

  D   They may not represent the actual values that employees believe are important

16 W Farm Ltd, a small farming company, has been delivering milk to a group of villages in the Yorkshire area for the last 80 years. Recently the owner, E, decided to create a mission statement for the company.

Which ONE of the following would be most appropriate for this business?

- A To increase turnover by 10% per annum for the next five years
- B To be the greatest company in the country
- C To provide high-quality milk for the community every day
- D To lobby the government for the rights of milk farmers everywhere

17 **Mission statements are usually based upon the organisation's current structure and position. This can then help to formulate the organisation's preferred, or ideal, future. This ideal future is typically communicated by which ONE of the following?**

- A Vision statement
- B Bottom-up budget
- C HRM plans
- D Business valuation

18 **Which THREE of the following are advantages of an organisation having a mission statement?**

- A Provides a basis for control of an organisation
- B Helps instil core values to staff
- C Is seen as a public-relations exercise
- D Improves communication with all stakeholders
- E Non-specific, allowing managers to choose whether to adopt it

19 **According to the SMART framework, which ONE of the following is a required feature of an objective?**

- A Sustainable
- B Strategic
- C Specific
- D Stakeholder-focused

OBJECTIVE TEST QUESTIONS : SECTION 1

20 HUH makes household furniture. The market is competitive and customers choose their furniture supplier by the quality of the manufacturer's products.

HUH has set itself the following objective:

'To produce perfect quality furniture.'

Which ONE of the following SMART criteria does HUH's objective meet?

- A   Attainable
- B   Timed
- C   Measurable
- D   Relevant

21 Yellowburn University, a not-for-profit higher education organisation, has the following mission statement:

'We aim to deliver excellent tuition in state of the art facilities to help develop socially responsible students and to contribute to global academic research.'

Which TWO of the following would be appropriate objectives to fit in with this mission?

- A   To deliver the best possible lessons
- B   Each member of staff is to write two research papers for publication over the next two years
- C   To increase car parking space at the university by 10% in the next 12 months to improve access
- D   To get 15% of all students to receive first class honours degrees each year
- E   To ensure 100% attendance from all students for every lecture

22 According to Braithwaite and Drahos, which THREE of the following 'actors' make up civil society?

- A   Knowledge based communities
- B   States
- C   Mass publics
- D   Organisations formed by firms
- E   Non-governmental organisations

23 The following diagram represents Mendelow's Power Interest matrix:

	Level of interest	
	Low	**High**
Power Low	A	B
Power High	C	D

Which ONE of the quadrants (A, B, C or D) on the above diagram represents stakeholders that need to be kept satisfied?

A   Quadrant A

B   Quadrant B

C   Quadrant C

D   Quadrant D

24 K plc is a large, multinational company that manufactures and sells motor vehicles. It has recently undertaken an analysis of its stakeholders using Mendelow's Power Interest matrix. During this analysis it has identified four stakeholders.

According to Mendelow's matrix, which of these four stakeholders should K adopt a 'keep informed' strategy towards in the following scenarios? Select ALL that apply.

A   **LPP – an international pressure group.** LPP is currently lobbying various national governments in an effort to reduce pollution – especially those from motor vehicles. LPP has arranged a number of high-profile protests in recent months, which have received a large amount of media attention. LPP is aware that K is about to launch a new model of motor car, which is large and consumes significant amounts of petrol.

B   **The government of country H.** Around three quarters of K plc's factories are based in country H. The government has enacted a number of new pieces of health and safety legislation for factory workers in the last several years. It undertakes regular unannounced checks of all factories in country H and has recently heavily fined one of K's rivals for failing to meet safety standards.

C   **K plc's sales staff.** K's sales staff make up around 25% of the total workforce. They are not significantly unionised and are relatively unskilled. They are all based in K's head office. K is considering reducing the number of sales staff by around a third as part of a cost-cutting exercise.

D   **F Ltd – a customer of K plc.** F Ltd runs a small chain of car retailers. They exclusively sell K plc's two-seater models of motor vehicles. F only represents around 0.5% of K plc's total sales. K is considering discontinuing the two-seater range in the near future.

OBJECTIVE TEST QUESTIONS : SECTION 1

25 **BetWalt, a medium-sized online gambling company, is to move all of its operations from the UK to a different country to reduce its cost base. In respect of this move, which ONE stakeholder group from the following list would need to be kept informed?**

   A   Low-skilled employees (not heavily unionised)

   B   Customers (both UK and abroad)

   C   UK government (BetWalt's move is not against local laws)

   D   Major institutional investors (with shareholdings of between 25% and 30% each)

26 Pirlo Pasta Ltd is a manufacturer of chilled ready meals for a large supermarket chain. It recently found that a batch of products had a different type of meat contained in the meals to that described on the packaging. The company immediately reported this to the food standards regulator – the Central Government Food Standards Agency (the CGFSA), as this was a breach of appropriate legislation, which could lead to heavy fines and penalties being levied on the company.

   The managing director of Pirlo identified, while undertaking stakeholder analysis using Mendelow's power-interest matrix, that the CGFSA had shifted from one stakeholder position to another.

   Which ONE of the following options correctly describes the shift in stakeholder position of the CGFSA?

   A   Key player to Keep informed

   B   Keep informed to Key player

   C   Keep satisfied to Keep informed

   D   Keep satisfied to Key player

27 RRL is a medium sized company that operates bus services throughout several major towns and cities. RRL has around 700 employees and around 85% of these employees are members of the OOB union. OOB is an active union and has regularly threatened RRL with strike action during disputes over employee pay and conditions.

   Which ONE of the following is the major source of stakeholder power that the OOB union has over RRL?

   A   Resource

   B   Expert

   C   System

   D   Positional

SUBJECT E3 : STRATEGIC MANAGEMENT

28 R is a national chain of supermarkets. It has recently purchased a large piece of land in the centre of a small, traditional fishing town with a view to building a large store. There has been significant resistance to this by local residents, but in response R has promised to create a sizeable amount of free car parking for residents, as well as investment in local sports and entertainment facilities.

According to Cyert and March, R is adopting which ONE of the following stakeholder conflict resolution strategies?

- A   Side payments
- B   Satisficing
- C   Exercise of power
- D   Sequential attention

29 **Which ONE of the following groups would an organisation consider when planning a non-market strategy?**

- A   Major customers
- B   Government regulators
- C   Key suppliers
- D   Large competitors

GOVERNANCE, ETHICS AND CORPORATE SOCIAL RESPONSIBILITY

30 **Which THREE of the following are common arguments FOR organisations adopting a strong approach to corporate social responsibility (CSR)?**

- A   Increased profitability due to short term cost reductions
- B   Faster strategic decision-making
- C   Improved reputation with environmentally conscious customers
- D   Ability to attract higher calibre staff
- E   Reduced chance of government intervention in the future

31 V is the Managing Director and part-owner of a chain of gyms. He currently pays his staff the minimum legal wage set by the national government, as well as offering them the minimum statutory holiday entitlement.

In recent months, V's gyms have suffered from significant staff turnover. Several key employees have moved to rival gyms and taken a large number of V's customers with them.

V has decided to adopt a further range of cost-cutting exercises in response to this. He has argued that he needs to maintain the profitability of the gyms for the benefit of himself and his business partners.

Which ONE of Johnson, Scholes and Whittington's ethical stances is V adopting?

A   Shaper of society

B   Long-term shareholder interest

C   Short-term shareholder interest

D   Multiple stakeholder obligation

32 X is Operations Director of a Y, a large organisation. X is responsible for a wide range of decisions, covering the procurement, production, sales and IT functions.

X is considering a supplier selection decision. One of the organisation's suppliers is a small, local company. It has supplied specialist components to Y for many years, and has always delivered on time and to a high level of quality. A large multinational has tendered to supply the same components at a much lower price than that offered by the local supplier. X knows that the local supplier may go out of business if he decides to buy from the multinational.

X decides to buy from the local supplier, justifying his decision on the grounds that while the multinational can supply more cheaply, delivery of the components from the multinational would increase the carbon footprint of Y. This would go against Y's published mission statement and objectives.

Johnson, Scholes and Whittington propose four 'ethical stances' that can be adopted by individuals or organisations. Which ONE of the following stances is being adopted by X?

A   Multiple stakeholder obligation

B   Short-term shareholder interest

C   Long-term shareholder interest

D   Shaper of society

33 Which TWO of the following statements regarding Corporate Social Responsibility (CSR), ethics and sustainability are correct?

A   To be successful, the ethical tone within the organisation needs to come from senior management

B   Sustainability refers to a firm's obligation to maximise its positive impact on stakeholders while minimising the negative effects

C   Management accountants have a responsibility to promote an ethical corporate culture

D   Sustainability and CSR will lead to cost savings, but only in the long-term

SUBJECT E3 : STRATEGIC MANAGEMENT

34 H operates a successful bakery. He has recently started recycling all waste generated by his store in response to government legislation. At the request of a local charity, he has also started donating any leftover food at the end of each day to a shelter for the homeless.

According to Carroll, which ONE of the following philosophies best describes H's actions?

  A Accommodation

  B Proaction

  C Reaction

  D Defence

35 Which THREE of the following are included within Carroll's four-part model of corporate social responsibility?

  A Stakeholder responsibility

  B Shareholder responsibility

  C Legal responsibility

  D Ethical responsibility

  E Economic responsibility

36 According to CIMA's report 'Evolution of corporate sustainability practices', there are ten elements of organisational sustainability. These are grouped under three headings.

For each of the following elements, identify which relevant heading they should be included under by placing them in the appropriate box.

Elements:

- Board and senior management commitment
- Champions to promote sustainability and celebrate success
- Extensive and effective sustainability training
- Ensuring sustainability is the responsibility of everyone within the organisation
- Including sustainability targets and objectives in performance appraisal.

Place each of the above elements into a box under the appropriate heading below.

Strategy and oversight	Execution and alignment	Performance and reporting

37 J is a CIMA Member, and Financial Controller of X, a large company manufacturing military equipment.

X is currently experiencing financial difficulties, though this is not public knowledge. The CEO of X is due to meet the Defence Minister of a foreign government which is known to be looking for new military equipment that X would be able to supply. The CEO has asked J to produce a PowerPoint presentation, summarising the financial position and forecast of X. The CEO has asked J to include a very optimistic forecast, as this will improve the chances of X securing a contract from the foreign government.

To do this would be in breach of the fundamental ethical principle (according to CIMA's Code of Ethics) of _____1_____.

Which ONE of the following options would correctly fill Gap 1?

A   Objectivity

B   Integrity

C   Confidentiality

D   Professional competence

38 H is a CIMA member, and Financial Controller of X plc, a large company manufacturing furniture.

X plc is currently looking for a new supplier of printed fabrics. Three suppliers are being considered, one of which is Y Ltd. Y Ltd is owned by Z, an old school friend of H. Z has asked H to 'put in a good word for Y Ltd' with the procurement manager of X plc. Z knows that H is good friends with X plc's procurement manager.

Which ONE of the following options would H be breaching by agreeing to Z's request?

A   Objectivity

B   Integrity

C   Confidentiality

D   Professional competence

39 P is a CIMA member, and Financial Controller of X plc, a large company manufacturing soap.

X plc is currently looking for a new supplier of packaging materials for its products. It has started a tendering process to help it pick between four possible suppliers. One of these potential suppliers is BRG – which is owned by a close personal friend of P. She has asked P to tell her what prices the other suppliers in the tender process have quoted X plc.

Which ONE of the following options would P be breaching by agreeing to his friend's request?

A   Objectivity

B   Integrity

C   Confidentiality

D   Professional competence

40 Professional accountants may have to follow a number of steps when attempting to resolve an ethical threat. These steps include:

- A Obtain advice from professional institutes
- B Establish ethical issues involved
- C Follow established internal procedures
- D Refer to relevant fundamental principles
- E Consider withdrawing from the engagement

Place these steps into the correct order, beginning with the earliest, by writing the letters A–E in the correct order.

41 Which THREE of the following are valid reasons for disclosing commercially sensitive information to a third party which would NOT breach the ethical principle of confidentiality?

- A It is required due to a professional, ethical dilemma
- B It is permitted by law and authorised by the client
- C It is required by law
- D Failure to disclose could materially disadvantage the third party
- E There is a professional duty or right to disclose the information

ANALYSING THE ORGANISATIONAL ECOSYSTEM – 20%

EXTERNAL ENVIRONMENTAL ANALYSIS

42 L Ltd is a small company which offers accountancy services to a range of clients. L is relatively new to the market and is considering undertaking formal environmental analysis.

Which of the following are purposes of L undertaking external environmental analysis? Select ALL that apply.

- A Allows L to assess its competition
- B Enables L to identify its resources
- C Allows L to gain a deeper understanding of its market
- D Enables L to understand its industry
- E Helps L to meet its stakeholder needs

43 X is a large logistics (parcel delivery) company. As part of its strategic planning process, X has identified several factors in its business environment that seem to be important. Categorise each factor according to PESTEL analysis.

There is increasing pressure on the logistics industry to minimise its carbon footprint. This should be classified as _____1_____.

The government is planning a change to employment law, to prevent drivers working more than ten hours in any 24 hour period. This should be classified as _____2_____.

The use of Global Positioning Systems (GPS) and smartphones are now becoming an industry threshold competence. This should be classified as _____3_____.

The current government is unpopular with voters, and there may be an election soon. X is unsure of the impact this would have on their business. This should be classified as _____4_____.

Use the options below to fill in the missing words in gaps 1 to 4.

A   Political

B   Economic

C   Legal

D   Social

E   Technological

F   Environmental

44 Which TWO of the following statements regarding PESTEL analysis are correct?

A   PESTEL analysis is becoming more difficult due to increasing volatility in the global market

B   PESTEL analysis is prone to bias, which can reduce its usefulness

C   PESTEL analysis focuses on analysing the industry that an organisation operates within

D   PESTEL analysis examines the internal and external issues faced by the organisation

45 H is a large vehicle manufacturing company in country F, which has recently decided to undertake environmental analysis.

Which ONE of the following factors would most likely be identified under the 'political' heading of a PESTEL analysis?

A   New CAD and CAM has recently become available for use in F's factories

B   Recycling is seen as being increasingly important by the residents of country F

C   Increased disposable income of consumers within country F

D   Changes in minimum wage legislation within country F

SUBJECT E3 : STRATEGIC MANAGEMENT

46 G supplies electronic components to the automobile industry by exporting from the home country in which it is currently based. G is considering opening a manufacturing base overseas in country X.

Recommend which THREE of the following are sources of information that G could use when evaluating potential countries to invest in.

- A Publications from the OECD and the World Bank
- B Automobile industry publications
- C G's financial statements
- D Amnesty International's human right record analysis for country X
- E G's current website

47 Which THREE of the following are forces within Porter's Five Forces model?

- A Threat of new entrants
- B Demand conditions
- C Power of buyers
- D Threat of substitutes
- E Political and legal

48 X is a marketing services company, providing consultancy to a range of business clients. As part of its strategic planning process, X has made several changes that seem to have had an impact on its business environment. Evaluate each factor according to Porter's Five Forces model analysis.

X and its rivals have managed to persuade the Government to require all marketing services companies to complete a time-consuming and bureaucratic registration process, and to comply with an industry code of conduct. This represents a decrease in _____1_____.

X has persuaded its entire staff to sign a new contract which prevents them for working for any rival company for a period of two years, should they resign. This represents a decrease in _____2_____.

Use the options below to fill in the missing words in gaps 1 and 2.

- A Competitive rivalry
- B Threat of new entrants
- C Power of customers
- D Power of suppliers
- E Threat of substitutes

OBJECTIVE TEST QUESTIONS : SECTION 1

49 Q is an electrical appliance manufacturer and currently specialises in the manufacture of domestic vacuum cleaners. Q operates in this market with four other companies. Each manufacturer similar products and sell similar volumes of vacuum cleaners each year.

Q and its rivals own a large number of patents relating to the manufacture of vacuum cleaners. Q buys its raw materials through a number of small suppliers, as do its rivals.

From the information above, which ONE of the following forces from Porter's Five Forces model would be classified as 'high'?

A   Threat of new entrants

B   Power of suppliers

C   Competitive rivalry

D   Threat of substitutes

50 Y offers consumer insurance products, including car and life insurance.

According to Porter's Five Forces model, which ONE of the following would indicate that the power of buyers in Y's industry is high?

A   Y's insurance policies have a number of special features, differentiating them from those offered by its rivals

B   Y has few rivals in the car and life insurance market

C   Y's customers typically use comparison websites to see how much their insurance would cost from a number of different suppliers

D   Y's customers are legally required to have car insurance

51 Z plc is using Porter's Five Forces model to examine the key aspects of the organisation's industry that may impact upon strategy. It has identified the following issues:

1   One of Z's customers is considering backwards integration of their supply chain.

2   Z plc and its rivals have secured exclusive agreements with all major distribution channels for their products.

3   Z has managed to achieve significant economies of scale in its manufacturing processes.

For each of the above issues Z has identified, decide which force(s) they relate to and whether the force is increased or decreased by placing the relevant issue number in the appropriate box below. Note: each box can be used more than once and each number can be placed in more than one box.

	Increased	Decreased
Power of customers		
Threat of substitutes		
Threat of new entrants		

17

52 OFG plc is a manufacturer of military hardware. It sells to a number of countries, although this is heavily regulated by the central government of its home country – country J. OFG feels that its major competitive advantage over its two major industry rivals is its strength in research and development. This is important given the fast-changing nature of its market. OFG has recently formed a joint venture with one of its rivals to develop a new weapons satellite system.

Which TWO of the following options are possible reasons why OFG would find the use of Porter's Five Forces model of limited use?

A   OFG has very few competitive rivals

B   OFG operates in a fast-moving industry

C   Porter's Five Forces assumes that rivals do not act collaboratively

D   The Five Forces model focuses solely on industry profitability

53 X is a company offering its customers broadband internet access. It sells to both residential customers as well as businesses.

X is considering a major investment in its IT systems, which it hopes will deliver a competitive advantage. The new systems will improve customer service levels, and reduce the cost of routine processes. Although the investment will cost several million dollars, X expects payback to be very fast. In the short term, X expects that excellent customer service will be a core competence. However, X accepts that its competitors will 'catch up' within five years, making excellent customer service a threshold competence.

Advise X which THREE of the competitive forces in its industry will be affected by this investment.

A   Threat of new entrants

B   Competitive rivalry

C   Threat of substitutes

D   Power of buyers

E   Power of suppliers

OBJECTIVE TEST QUESTIONS : SECTION 1

54 Pink is a distributor of garden furniture (chairs, tables, parasols, loungers) which it sells wholesale to a wide range of retailers such as specialist stores and hypermarkets.

The Board of Pink is currently analysing its business environment and has noticed that some of its larger customers are automating their procurement and inbound logistics processes by using 'bots'. At present, Pink does not have any automated processes in its outbound logistics or marketing and sales functions. The Board is not aware that any of Pink's rivals are yet using, or planning to use, bots in those functions. The Board is understandably concerned by the adoption of new technologies by customers and wishes to understand the threat that they pose to Pink's competitive strategy.

Analyse the above information and identify which of Porter's 'Five Forces', as they relate to Pink, is/are likely to have been affected by the change noticed by the Board. Select ALL that apply.

- A Threat of new entrants
- B Threat of substitutes
- C Competitive rivalry
- D Power of suppliers
- E Power of customers

55 D plc manufactures a range of products, including the TT155. The TT155 was seen as being extremely innovative on its launch two years ago and has experienced high sales growth. Its sales growth, while still high, has fallen in recent months due to a number of rivals launching products similar to the TT155. D has started investing in advertising (as well as legal action against some rivals for copying patented design features of the TT155). This has led to the TT155 experiencing relatively low profitability.

Which stage of the product life cycle is the TT155 currently within?

- A Growth
- B Decline
- C Maturity
- D Introduction

56 Price cutting and reduced promotion are typical strategies at which stage of the product life cycle?

- A Decline
- B Growth
- C Introduction
- D Maturity

57 Going-rate pricing would be most common at which stage of the product life cycle?

- A Introduction
- B Maturity
- C Decline
- D Growth

SUBJECT E3 : STRATEGIC MANAGEMENT

58 L manufactures and sells high quality tents for use by campers. Y manufactures and sells high quality caravans. L and Y are aware that they are trying to sell to the same customer segments.

According to competitor analysis theory, what type of competitors are L and Y?

A   Generic

B   Industry

C   Brand

D   Form

59 ABC is a manufacturer of portable communications equipment. The equipment is designed to be used in toxic environments. ABC has identified four main competitors and wishes to classify them.

	Competitor		Type of competitor
A	A firm which makes a similar product, but for a different market segment (for the nuclear industry)	1	Brand
B	A firm which creates a similar product to ABC and tries to sell it to ABC's customers	2	Generic
C	A firm which competes for the same income as ABC (e.g. safety equipment)	3	Industry
D	A firm which attempts to meet the same needs as ABC, but with a different product (e.g. flare guns)	4	Form

Identify which type of competitor correlates to each of the competitors identified by pairing the appropriate letter and number (e.g. A1, B2, etc).

60 YU is undertaking detailed competitor analysis and is developing a series of competitor response profiles.

One of YU's major rivals is GG. GG's response to YU's previous strategies has varied significantly. When YU launched a new product last year, GG responded with an aggressive pricing policy on its own products. However, when YU recently launched a major advertising campaign, GG did not respond at all. YU has been unable to see a pattern to GG's actions.

According to competitor analysis theory, which ONE of the following competitor response styles best fits GG?

A   Laid back

B   Selective

C   Stochastic

D   Tiger

OBJECTIVE TEST QUESTIONS : SECTION 1

61 X is a multinational car manufacturer, based in Country Y.

As part of its strategic planning process, X is considering further overseas expansion, and wishes to determine whether being based in Country Y gives it a competitive advantage over domestic car manufacturers in other countries.

Country Y has two main universities, each of which offers a degree programme in automotive engineering. The graduates from this programme are very highly regarded and are seen as being important to X's operations.

The graduates produced by the local university are an example of which ONE factor from Michael Porter's 'Diamond' model?

A   Factor conditions

B   Related and supporting industries

C   Demand conditions

D   Strategy, structure and rivalry

62 V is a multinational motor vehicle manufacturer, based in Country O.

As part of its strategic planning process, V is considering further overseas expansion, and wishes to determine whether being based in Country O gives it a competitive advantage over domestic car manufacturers in other countries.

When V was formed, fifty years ago, there were eight car manufacturers based in Country O. There are now only two, following a series of acquisitions by V and its rival, and a number of bankruptcies. V competes aggressively against its rival, both in terms of price and quality.

This represents an example of which ONE factor from Michael Porter's 'Diamond' model?

A   Demand conditions

B   Related and supporting industries

C   Factor conditions

D   Strategy, structure and rivalry

63 SP Ltd operates a chain of jewellers in country H. It is currently planning to expand into country G.

Which THREE of the following would be classified as 'related and supporting industries' for SP Ltd within country G when using Porter's Diamond model?

A   Country G has a large number of existing chains of jewellers

B   Country G has a large number of suppliers of precious metals

C   Country G has a large number of unemployed residents

D   Country G has a large number of shop fitting businesses and decorators

E   Country G has a large number of firms providing security services

SUBJECT E3 : STRATEGIC MANAGEMENT

64 HGY is a chain of opticians which is considering expanding into country F. It has decided to analyse the decision using Porter's Diamond model.

Consider the following lists of issues relating to HGY's proposed expansion as well as the dimensions of Porter's Diamond.

	Issue		Dimension
A	High levels of poor eyesight in country F	1	Factor conditions
B	HGY has a monopoly in its home country	2	Demand conditions
C	Large amount of empty premises in country F	3	Strategy, structure and rivalry
D	No suppliers of eye testing equipment in country F	4	Related and supporting industries

Identify which issue relates to each dimension by pairing the appropriate letter and number (e.g. A1, B2, etc).

65 Grace is a large car manufacturer, based in South America. As part of its strategic planning process, Grace has been scanning its business ecosystem.

Grace has noticed that, while many cars are connected to the Internet by online applications ('apps') to provide location, traffic and service information, some are now being personalised. Drivers receive content and services that are unique to them, such as the location of the nearest branch their favourite coffee chain. These apps 'learn', and modify output based on the driver's use of the app.

The consultancy group Accenture wrote a report, in 2015, called "Accenture Technology Vision". This report highlighted 5 emerging trends, which were shaping the digital landscape for organisations, on which business leaders should focus when developing digital strategies.

Analyse the above description, and identify which of the trends is evidenced in the business ecosystem of Grace.

A   The Internet of Me

B   The Platform (r)evolution

C   Outcome economy

D   The intelligent enterprise

OBJECTIVE TEST QUESTIONS : **SECTION 1**

STRATEGIC NETWORKS AND PLATFORMS

66 AAA is a specialist car manufacturer, based in G, a country in Europe. AAA manufactures most of the components of its car in-house. The main exception is the car's engine, which AAA buys from a major car manufacturer and then sends them all to a single, highly specialised company (BBB) for modification and upgrades. While the engine is relatively expensive, it is the work of BBB that represents the single most significant cost of producing each car. AAA has, on occasions, paid BBB the equivalent of 25% of the final sales price of a car. The sales manager has stated BBB's work is one of the cars 'unique selling points'.

Based on the above information, evaluate the strength of the bargaining power of suppliers at AAA. (Select ONE of the following options).

A   Strong

B   Average

C   Weak

D   Very weak

67 H bakes and sells bread and other wheat-based baked goods. It is currently undertaking detailed supply chain management and has identified a number of partner organisations that form its supply chain.

Which THREE of the following organisations would form part of H's downstream supply chain?

A   Farmers

B   Consumers

C   Supermarkets

D   Wheat wholesalers

E   Small, independent food retailers

68 QII is an electronics manufacturer. It produces circuit boards for many other retailers and is the largest single user of palladium – a rare metal – in the world. QII purchases its palladium from two specialist companies who process palladium which they, in turn, have purchased from palladium mines around the world. Palladium prices are volatile and QII have typically been able to negotiate a low price for the metal they purchase due to their significant buying power.

QII has recently started an analysis of its supply chain and one of its managers has suggested that the company monitor the cash flow and profitability of all QII's upstream and downstream partners.

Which ONE of the following reasons would best justify the manager's suggestion?

A   To ensure future supply and demand for QII's circuit boards

B   To ensure high quality of QII's raw materials

C   To maximise QII's ability to collaborate with customers regarding circuit board design

D   To ensure QII is able to gather as much information about its supply chain as possible

69 KKB is a company which operates passenger trains in country G. It has been granted an exclusive ten-year franchise by the government of country G to run trains in the East of the country. It is considering launching an e-procurement system for its purchases of diesel (necessary for the running of around 45% of its trains). There are a number of suppliers of diesel, though KKB has historically only ordered diesel from one of these (using a manual ordering system). Diesel prices vary significantly between suppliers and on the open market.

Storage of diesel is expensive, but KKB has been forced to keep a significant amount in inventory as its current supplier cannot always guarantee prompt delivery.

Which of the following statements relating to KKB's e-procurement system is correct? (Select ALL that apply).

A   It will increase KKB's competitive advantage in its market

B   It will reduce KKB's over-reliance on a single supplier

C   It will enable KKB to reduce its inventory holding costs

D   It will reduce KKB's exposure to technology risk

70 GHO is a company that rents motorbikes and scooters to individuals through a small chain of stores.

In order to improve customer service levels, The Marketing Director (MD) has told the Marketing Manager (MM) that she must change the marketing approach from 'transactions marketing' to 'relationship marketing'. The MM is unsure what the MD means, and has asked for your advice.

Place the following characteristics of relationship and transactions marketing into the correct category in the table below.

- Concentrates on products
- Service quality is a critical success factor
- Requires detailed knowledge of customer needs
- Motorbike and scooter quality is a critical success factor
- Little emphasis on repeat rental

Transaction marketing	Relationship marketing

OBJECTIVE TEST QUESTIONS : SECTION 1

71 Which THREE of the following are included within Payne's six markets model?

  A   Customer markets

  B   Transaction markets

  C   Internal markets

  D   Public markets

  E   Influence markets

72 VVC is a television broadcaster in country B. Much of its revenue comes from advertising sponsors who will pay higher fees for their adverts if the number of people watching VVC's television programmes rises.

VVC has recently been informed of a new mobile application that large numbers of people in country B are using. Individuals download the application to their mobile phone and it gives them tailored suggestions as to the best programmes to watch on television each day.

According to Payne's six markets model, which ONE of VVC's six markets would this new application be classified within?

  A   Customer

  B   Influence

  C   Internal

  D   Recruitment

73 ABC has just made a financial loss on trading for the first time in 50 years. ABC's senior management is therefore currently undertaking a customer review.

The Management accountant has discovered the following statistics about three of the company's largest customers. For each customer he identified the number of times a sales assistant had to visit the customer, and the number of rush deliveries that ABC had to provide for each customer. In order to stay competitive, ABC cannot pass on the cost of either of these activities to its customers.

	Customer 1	Customer 2	Customer 3
Number of sales visits made	56	34	258
Sales Revenue	58	24	85
Number of rush deliveries made	5	20	163

Which ONE of the following statements best describes the current issue at AAA?

  A   All three customers are earning revenue for ABC, so the company should not make any changes to the way it manages them

  B   ABC should stop undertaking expensive rush deliveries for all customers

  C   ABC needs to increase the selling price to all three customers due to the number of rush deliveries

  D   Despite Customer 3 providing the most revenue, it is not necessarily earning the highest margin

SUBJECT E3 : STRATEGIC MANAGEMENT

74 Residents of country U eat large amounts of food from takeaways each year. These are small, usually family owned, restaurants that cook food and then deliver them to the customer's home, typically for a small fee. Many of these restaurants have no web presence and only accept cash payments. Unfortunately, many customers now wish to be able to order online and pay by credit card, as the use of cash becomes less popular.

HGH has recently launched a new website. This allows customers to browse the menus of nearby takeaways, and place online orders, which HGH then communicates to the takeaway. HGH accepts card payments from customers and then transfers these funds directly into the takeaway owner's bank account.

HGH's website is an example of which ONE of the following?

A   Intermediation

B   Countermediation

C   Disintermediation

D   Reintermediation

75 JAF sells cosmetics to individual consumers through a chain of stores in every major town and city in country H.

Which TWO of the following are suitable examples of downstream supply chain management for JAF?

A   Set-up of electronic data interchange (EDI) between JAF and its customers

B   Introduction of customer loyalty cards for shoppers

C   E-procurement of make-up by JAF

D   Data warehousing and mining of JAF customer information

76 Q operates a pub in the capital of country G, serving a range of premium alcoholic drinks. Drinks can be extremely expensive, with the average margin around five times higher than a typical pub. Q has identified that the majority of its customers view attending this pub as a way of showing their colleagues that they earn a large sum of money.

According to Maslow's hierarchy of needs, which ONE of the following needs is Q's pub fulfilling for its users?

A   Self-fulfilment

B   Ego

C   Social

D   Physiological

77 F has recently purchased a new mobile phone manufactured by OOL plc. However, one week after the purchase she discovered that a new model of mobile phone had been released by one of OOL plc's rivals. This new model had more features than the one she had bought, leading her to regret her purchase of one of OOL's mobile phones.

Which ONE of the following is F experiencing?

- A   Cognitive dissonance
- B   Reciprocal buying
- C   Propensity modelling
- D   Transaction marketing

RESOURCES AND VALUE CREATION WITHIN THE ORGANISATIONAL ECOSYSTEM

78 QG has a sophisticated database which its managers use to identify individual customer needs as well as market trends. Since its creation, the database has helped boost QG's sales by around 25%.

Which ONE of the following resource classifications would QG's database be included within?

- A   Make-up
- B   Management
- C   Management information
- D   Markets

79 The following statements relate to organisational resources and competences. Select ALL of the statements that are correct.

- A   Core competences are difficult for an organisation's rivals to imitate
- B   Threshold competences give competitive advantage to the organisation
- C   Core competences are often intangible in nature
- D   Threshold competences tend to turn into core competences over time
- E   'Core competences' and 'critical success factors' have the same meaning

80 X is a car and van rental company. It provides short-term and long-term rental of vehicles to corporate and private customers, to satisfy an immediate need (such as moving house, or having a vehicle off the road for repair) or a continuing need (such as a busy period, where more capacity is needed).

X is part-way through its first formal strategic planning process, and has developed a mission statement:

'X aims to be the first choice vehicle rental company, by providing well-maintained vehicles at an affordable price, and excellent customer service.'

X has developed eight performance measures, based on this mission, but is uncertain how to categorise those measures into critical success factors (CSFs) and key performance indicators (KPIs).

Measures:

1 High levels of customer satisfaction
2 Answer telephone calls within five rings
3 Vehicle breakdowns happen less than 1 per 100 rental days
4 Prices must be within 5% of the average charge by rivals
5 Affordable rental charges
6 No more than 2% of customers submit complaints
7 Well-maintained vehicles
8 Excellent customer service

For each of the above measures, identify which are CSFs and which KPI it is related to by placing the relevant measure number in the appropriate box below.

CSF	Related KPI

OBJECTIVE TEST QUESTIONS : SECTION 1

81 C is a mobile telecommunications company. It provides a network, through which calls can be routed, and enters into agreements with mobile telephone users. Some of the users buy call time, messages and data in advance ('pay and go'), while others pay a fixed amount each month in return for a package of calls, messages and data, with a limit set for each ('contract').

C is part-way through its first formal strategic planning process, and has developed a mission statement:

'C aims to provide consistently clear calls, at a reasonable price, to happy and loyal customers.'

C has developed a series of performance measures, based on the mission, but is uncertain how to categorise those measures into critical success factors (CSFs) and key performance indicators (KPIs).

Measures:

1. Reasonable prices
2. An average score of 4.5 out of 5 (or higher) on customer satisfaction surveys
3. Customer loyalty
4. Less than 1 in 50 calls should fail due to network problems
5. Happy customers
6. Good quality network provision
7. 90% customer retention at the end of their contract
8. Average contract charges to be lower than that of two largest rivals

For each of the above measures, identify which are CSFs and which KPI it is related to by placing the relevant measure number in the appropriate box below.

CSF	Related KPI

82 B Ltd has identified a critical success factor (CSF) for its organisation:

'Have an excellent quality product.'

Which ONE of the following would be the most suitable key performance indicator for this CSF?

- A Reduce the number of defects identified by quality control and customers by 25%
- B Reduce the average time taken to deal with complaints about quality by 20%
- C Increase quality by 15% over the next year
- D Increase the amount of quality training for manufacturing staff

83 S is attempting to decide the critical success factors (CSFs) for his business.

According to Rockart's model, which THREE of the following options are sources of CSFs?

A   The wider environment

B   The company itself and its situation within its industry

C   The industry the business is in

D   The stakeholders of the business

E   The operational systems of the company

84 V plc is a national bank based in country Y. It has recently been informed by the national government that it is being fined a large sum of money for misleading customers.

V is aware that the fine will place a strain on its cash-flows for the coming year (V usually has a large cash surplus each year), meaning that it needs to introduce a new critical success factor (CSF) of 'maximising cash-flows' for the coming year as a one-off target.

According to Rockart's model, which ONE of the following sources of CSFs is being described?

A   The company itself and its situation within its industry

B   The industry the business is in

C   Temporal factors

D   The wider environment

85 'A workshop which mobilises resources to solve specific problems.'

This is a definition of which ONE of the following concepts?

A   Value linkage

B   Value system

C   Value shop

D   Value driver

86 **Which THREE of the following options are SECONDARY (or support) activities within Porter's Value Chain?**

A   Infrastructure

B   Procurement

C   Service

D   Marketing and sales

E   Technology development

OBJECTIVE TEST QUESTIONS : SECTION 1

87 QOI prints and sells dictionaries. The Managing Director of QOI has recently made a statement relating to QOI's performance with regards to Porter's Value Chain model.

'QOI's inbound logistics processes are excellent as we regularly manage to find the most cost effective paper suppliers by regular scanning of the market. Our operations are highly efficient, with high quality automated printing systems in our factory. Our outbound logistics are also well designed, which I can attribute to our strong promotions and excellent advertising.'

Which ONE of the following statements best describes the Managing Director's level of understanding of the Value Chain model?

A EXCELLENT – he has shown that he understands all of the activities he discussed

B GOOD – he has misunderstood one of the activities he discussed

C POOR – he has misunderstood two of the activities he discussed

D VERY POOR – he has misunderstood all of the activities he discussed

88 F is a manufacturer of children's toys.

F is part-way through its first formal strategic planning process, and has tried to identify those activities it performs that its customers really seem to appreciate. The next step F must perform is to classify these activities using Porter's 'Value Chain' model.

Consider the following lists of activities within X and various Value Chain classifications.

	Activity		Value Chain classification
A	Handling customer complaints	1	Human resource management
B	Budgeting for the manufacturing process	2	Inbound logistics
C	Staff training	3	Infrastructure
D	Automated inventory control for raw material	4	Service

Identify which activity relates to each dimension by pairing the appropriate letter and number (e.g. A1, B2, etc).

89 JJE makes and sells freshly baked bread. It has recently developed an automated inventory control system for its finished loaves, which significantly reduces wastage.

Which ONE of the following Value Chain activities will JJE's automated inventory system directly improve?

A Procurement

B Outbound logistics

C Operations

D Inbound logistics

90 QHQ is a law firm. It has recently undertaken an analysis of its activities, but is uncertain which activity relates to each part of the firm's Value Chain.

Consider the following lists of activities within QHQ and various Value Chain classifications.

	Activity		Value Chain classification
A	Dealing with claims of negligence by customers	1	Inbound logistics
B	Attending court cases	2	Infrastructure
C	Central control systems that ensure each case is independently reviewed	3	Service
D	Receiving and storing data from client meetings	4	Operations

Identify which activity relates to each dimension by pairing the appropriate letter and number (e.g. A1, B2, etc).

91 YF is a call centre linked to the National Health Service in country A. When a patient calls YF, a medically qualified operator gathers information about their condition, which is entered onto a central database. This is used to make a decision about the cause of the patient's problem. The operator will then inform the patient about what to do next – i.e. whether they need to go to a hospital or a doctor's surgery. For non-emergencies, the operator will email this information to the patient for their future reference.

YF is considering the launch of a new expert IT system. This will allow operators to input detailed patient symptoms into the system, which will then make suggestions as to possible diagnoses in order to support the operator's decision-making process.

Which ONE of the following activities within YF's value chain is the new IT system supporting?

 A   Service

 B   Operations

 C   Outbound logistics

 D   Procurement

92 **Which THREE of the following options are activities within the 'Value Shop' model?**

 A   Procurement

 B   Choosing among solutions

 C   Operations

 D   Execution and control

 E   Development of opportunities

OBJECTIVE TEST QUESTIONS : SECTION 1

93 Be-a-Sport Ltd is a medium sized sports retailer. It currently operates three shops in city centre locations. The management team have a very careful recruitment policy; any applicant must have a 'passion for sport'.

Which ONE of the following would best describe the Value adding activity occurring at Be-a-Sport?

- A Marketing
- B Operations
- C Outbound logistics
- D Human Resource Management

94 QOS is a marketing consultancy business. QOS's most recent corporate analysis has identified that three new businesses have recently entered its market and started aggressively targeting QOS's key clients.

Which ONE of the following categories would these new business entrants to the market be classified within, as part of QOS's corporate appraisal?

- A Strength
- B Threat
- C Weakness
- D Opportunity

95 X is a public utility, generating and distributing electricity. Until last year, X was publicly owned. X was then privatised, and is now owned by a range of institutional investors, and a large number of private individuals.

When X was owned by the State, the mission of X was 'to provide continuity of electricity supply, at affordable prices'. The strategic planning process is managed by Y, a senior manager in the finance function. Y recognises that X now has to start planning for long term shareholder value. She believes that the market for utilities has changed significantly, and that there are many opportunities to use new technology, respond to customer needs, and add new products and services to the portfolio of X. Y believes that, unless X responds to changes in the business environment, it will be unable to satisfy stakeholders' expectations, particularly those of the institutional investors.

Y is in the process of carrying out the 'strategic analysis' activities of its planning process. Which of the following should be classified as 'strengths' of X, in a SWOT analysis (corporate appraisal)? (Select ALL correct answers)

- A The market for utilities has changed significantly
- B X generates and distributes electricity
- C The privatisation of X took place last year
- D X has sophisticated systems for identifying and repairing power outages
- E Y recognises that X now has to start planning for long-term shareholder value

96 A is a management accountant in G Ltd. She has been asked to prepare a presentation to senior management regarding the benefits and drawbacks of corporate appraisal (SWOT analysis). She has asked you to look over her notes, which included the following section of bullet points:

- Corporate appraisal is designed to focus on the industry that the company operates within and assess the major industry-wide factors that may affect our strategy.

- Corporate appraisal typically summarises the key issues identified by other analysis models, such as PEST and Porter's Five Forces.

- The corporate appraisal is a useful way of analysing the organisation's strategic capabilities, as well as the key issues it faces.

Which ONE of the following statements best describes A's level of understanding of corporate appraisal (SWOT)?

A   EXCELLENT – all three bullet points in her notes are correct

B   GOOD – only one of the bullet points in her notes is incorrect

C   POOR – two of the bullet points in her notes are incorrect

D   VERY POOR – all of the bullet points in her notes are incorrect

97 PAG is undertaking a position audit. The company makes and sells chairs and sofas and has a strong reputation within the market for quality at reasonable prices. PAG has identified that there is a growing market for office chairs. While PAG does not currently make this type of chair, their manufacture should use similar skills and raw materials to their current product line.

PAG's management has suggested a possible strategy of expansion into the office chair market. Which ONE of the following types of position audit strategy would this relate to?

A   Opportunity focusing on weakness

B   Threat focusing on strength

C   Threat focusing on weakness

D   Opportunity focusing on strength

98 **Which ONE of the following types of position audit strategy would typically be given top priority by an organisation?**

A   Threats focusing on weakness

B   Opportunity focusing on weakness

C   Threat focusing on strength

D   Opportunity focusing on strength

GENERATING STRATEGIC OPTIONS – 15%

FRAMEWORK FOR GENERATING STRATEGIC OPTIONS

99 Consider the following diagram. T represents the organisation's desired future position. F_0 represents the future performance from current operations, F_1 represents future performance after efficiency savings have been made and F_2 represents future performance after new strategic initiatives have been undertaken.

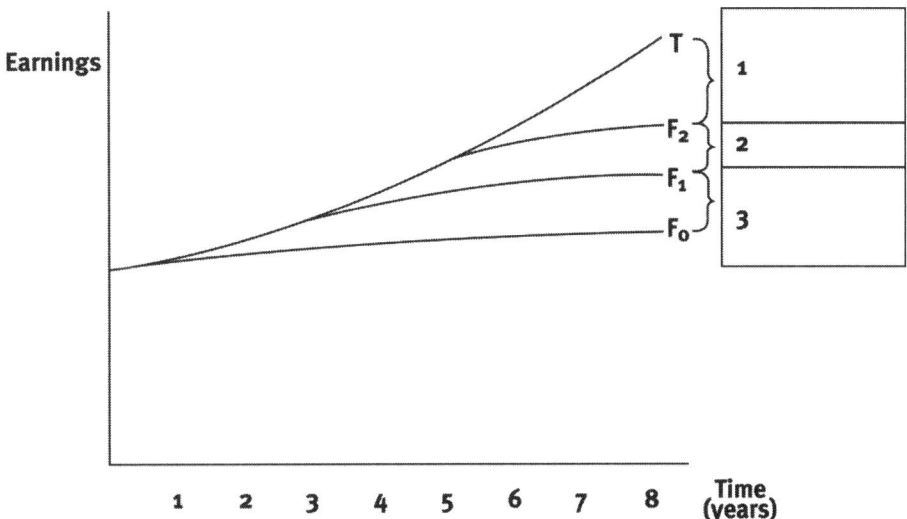

Identify which of the three gaps labelled on the diagram above is known as the 'expansion' gap.

A   Gap 1

B   Gap 2

C   Gap 3

100 WA is currently undertaking gap analysis. It wishes to start an effectiveness drive in order to close an expansion gap that has been identified.

Which TWO of the following strategies would be part of a typical effectiveness drive?

A   Price cuts to the product to boost sales volume

B   Sourcing cheaper raw materials for the production process

C   Increased automation to lower production costs

D   Development of new products for WA's existing markets

SUBJECT E3 : STRATEGIC MANAGEMENT

101 CHA is attempting to develop its ability to accurately forecast the changes in its market and its likely future industry position. It has assembled a panel of experts to help with its forecasting exercise, but wishes to avoid them influencing each other's opinion. The company has therefore decided to interrogate each expert using a series of questionnaires – thus ensuring the experts never meet.

Which ONE of the following forecasting methods has CHA adopted?

A   Think tank

B   Brainstorming

C   Delphi model

D   Derived demand

102 According to Irvine and Martin's 5Cs model, which THREE of the following are advantages of an organisation developing foresight?

A   Communication

B   Commitment

C   Concentration

D   Connection

E   Capability

103 WEJ is a mining company, which specialises in the extraction and processing of palladium and gold – two metals that are widely used in electronic devices. WEJ wishes to forecast the future market demand for these metals and believes that the only way to do this is to attempt to estimate the future global demand for electronic devices.

Which ONE of the following forecasting methods would WEJ find most appropriate to accomplish this?

A   Brainstorming

B   Derived demand

C   Think tank

D   Relevance trees

104 Scenario planning involves a number of distinct stages. These include:

A   Monitor reality to see which scenario is unfolding

B   Cluster together different factors to identify various consistent futures

C   Identify high-impact, high-uncertainty factors in the environment

D   Write the scenario

E   For each factor, identify different possible futures

F   For each scenario, identify and assess possible courses of action

G   Revise scenarios and strategic options as appropriate

Place these stages into the correct order, beginning with the earliest, by writing the letters A-G in the correct order.

105 IOS is currently starting to undertake scenario planning. It has begun by identifying a number of factors that it may wish to build into its scenarios.

Which TWO of the following factors would IOS be most likely to include in its scenario planning process?

- A   IOS's home country has recently elected a new government. It is not yet clear if they will introduce new legislation to increase minimum wages. This would have a major impact on IOS's profitability.
- B   IOS has recently been convicted of breaching several key health and safety laws in its factory. Based on similar cases brought against its rivals, IOS expects to be fined around 5% of its turnover. IOS has insurance in place that will cover this fine.
- C   IOS relies on a regular supply of gold as this is a key component within its products. The price of gold varies significantly on the open market and tends to rise sharply in times of recession. IOS is concerned that its product may become unprofitable if gold prices rise more than 25% from their current levels, but is uncertain about whether this would happen – even if a recession does occur.
- D   IOS is uncertain about whether it can retain its CEO in the long term. IOS has had a number of CEO's over the last ten years – each of them staying very different lengths of time in their roles. Fortunately, IOS has a well skilled Board of Directors and the change in CEOs has had little impact on the business in the past.

106 **Which THREE of the following are disadvantages of an organisation undertaking scenario planning?**

- A   May be costly and inaccurate
- B   May create scenarios that never actually occur
- C   Encourages risk-taking by management
- D   Creation of self-fulfilling prophecies
- E   Discourages creative thinking

107 You have recently read an article about game theory in a student magazine. The article had the following first paragraph:

'Game theory is concerned with the interrelationships between the competitive moves of a set of competitors. The common application of this is the so-called 'prisoner's dilemma' which indicates that competing companies often adopt strategies that leave them all worse off unless some level of collusion occurs between them.'

Which ONE of the following statements best describes the quality of the first paragraph of the student magazine article?

- A   EXCELLENT – there are no mistakes in the article's first paragraph
- B   GOOD – there is only one mistake regarding game theory in the magazine's first paragraph
- C   POOR – there are two mistakes regarding game theory in the magazine's first paragraph
- D   VERY POOR – all of the points made relating to game theory in the magazine's first paragraph are incorrect

SUBJECT E3: STRATEGIC MANAGEMENT

108 VAGH is a large house-building company. It is considering purchasing a section of land within a major town. The land is currently owned by the local government, who wishes VAGH to build two hundred new houses. VAGH has calculated that the net present value (NPV) of the project is negative. However, undertaking the building work would lead to VAGH being able to get preferential status for more profitable work with the local government in the future.

Which ONE of the following real options is included within the house-building project?

- A Option to abandon
- B Option to delay
- C Option to follow on
- D Option to return

109 Which of the following statements regarding real options is correct? Select ALL that apply.

- A Options to abandon are especially useful for projects with a large capital investment and an uncertain outcome.
- B An option to abandon a project will increase in value as the project becomes increasingly uncertain.
- C Options to delay refer to projects will that provide the business with access to other, more profitable projects in the future (i.e. after a given delay).
- D Generally, options fall in value as their duration falls.

STRATEGIC OPTIONS

110 JAV is a business which makes and sells laptop computers in country F. In recent years it has been struggling to compete with its rivals and has seen a significant fall in its market share. JAV's managers have decided to select a new business strategy based on Porter's Generic Strategies model.

After careful analysis, JAV identified that it lacked any real market research, which meant that the company was unable to obtain reliable information on the various individual segments of the laptop market in country F. JAV's managers felt that obtaining this information would be too costly and slow, meaning that JAV would be unable to adopt a _____1_____ strategy.

JAV's managers did, however, identify that the majority of products launched by JAV's rivals were high-specification, with good quality materials and many innovative design features. Products with inferior quality, such as those sold by JAV have not sold well in country F. This information led JAV's management team to decide that the best generic strategy to adopt for the company was _____2_____.

Use the options below to fill in the missing words in gaps 1 and 2.

- A Differentiation
- B Cost leadership
- C Focus

OBJECTIVE TEST QUESTIONS : SECTION 1

111 TIDL plc, a UK based supermarket, has adopted a strategy of cost leadership. TIDL wish to be the lowest average cost producer in the UK.

Which of the following THREE benefits would TIDL expect to gain?

- A   Higher profits as TIDL can charge the same price as their competitors yet earn a better margin
- B   Increased reputation
- C   Cost leadership allows for price penetration strategy to be enacted
- D   Allows TIDL to defend itself in a price war
- E   Allows TIDL to focus on a small customer base

112 Spiral Ltd is a small company based H Country in a region known for its hill walking. Spiral sell specialist walking equipment in their small shop at the foot of the mountains. They do not have a website, yet are able to sell their products at premium prices.

Which of the following ONE of Porter's generic strategies best fits Spiral Ltd?

- A   Cost leadership
- B   Differentiation
- C   Focus – Cost leadership
- D   Focus – Differentiation

113 SOC is a supermarket in country H. The supermarket industry in country H is saturated, with large numbers of chains of supermarkets in all segments of the market.

SOC has at least five major rivals in the market, each with a similar market size to SOC.

SOC has already undertaken significant efficiency strategies to bring its cost base down to match those of its rivals. It does not feel that it is possible to reduce these core costs down further for SOC or its rivals.

SOC and its rivals each offer branded and unbranded food items. SOC and its rivals charge similar prices for these items. None of the supermarkets offer non-food items.

According to Porter's generic strategies model, SOC would be an example of an organisation that is (select ONE of the following options):

- A   A differentiator
- B   A cost leader
- C   Stuck in the middle
- D   A niche-player (a focus approach has been adopted)

114 CHO is considering designing and launching a new range of smartphones which are specifically tailored to the over 60s. The phones will have a large, bright display and CHO intends to ensure that they are extremely user-friendly. CHO is aware that there is nothing like this currently being sold on the market.

Smartphone uptake has been very slow in CHO's market amongst the over 60s, with nearly all smartphones sold by CHO and its rivals being purchased by customers under the age of 30.

Many of the over 60s in CHO's market are on relatively low fixed incomes, in many cases with government pensions, and have relatively little disposable income.

Which THREE of the following are risks that CHO may face when adopting this focus strategy?

A The market for the over 60s may not be large enough to support the investment required to develop the Smartphone

B CHO has little experience of selling to the over 60s, or knowledge of what this niche wants from a Smartphone

C CHO can charge a premium for its new product as it is tailored specifically to the needs of the over 60s market segment

D CHO will face little competition in the over 60s market segment, as there are no similar products on the market

E CHO may find its market for the new phone shrinks significantly if, for example, inflation rates rise, leading to a fall in disposable income

115 The following diagram represents Ansoff's product/market growth matrix.

		Products	
		Existing	New
Markets	Existing	1	2
	New	3	4

According to Ansoff's model, which ONE of the above quadrants relates to a 'market development' strategy?

A Quadrant 1

B Quadrant 2

C Quadrant 3

D Quadrant 4

116 HUT sells board games, including one known as 'Housopoly'. Housopoly was once one of the most popular board games that HUT sold, but it has recently entered a period of decline. HUT has therefore updated the packaging of the board game, as well as slightly reducing its selling price.

According to Ansoff's product/market matrix, which of the following strategies has HUT adopted?

A   Market development

B   Product development

C   Diversification

D   Market penetration

117 MAH sells clothing, homewares and food through a large number of city-centre high-street stores across country U. It does not currently have an online presence.

It has recently initiated a number of different strategies and it wishes to categorise them using Ansoff's product/market matrix.

Consider the following lists of strategies within MAH as well as Ansoff's matrix classifications.

	MAH strategy		Ansoff classification
A	MAH has started selling selected food products in motorway service stations across country U	1	Market penetration
B	MAH has launched a major new advertising campaign for its current clothes ranges, under the slogan 'MAH for all'	2	Diversification
C	MAH is piloting selling domestic electricals through its existing retail stores	3	Product development
D	MAH has considered selling selected banking services on the internet	4	Market development

Identify which activity relates to each dimension by pairing the appropriate letter and number (e.g. A1, B2, etc).

118 VAT is a large supermarket chain. It is considering the purchase of a number of farms that provide VAT with a significant amount of its fresh produce. VAT feels that by purchasing the farms it will have greater control over its supply chain.

Which ONE of the following types of diversification is VAT undertaking?

A   Forward vertical

B   Backwards vertical

C   Horizontal

D   Conglomerate

SUBJECT E3 : STRATEGIC MANAGEMENT

119 SAD is considering diversifying into an unrelated market. Which TWO of the following reasons are likely reasons that SAD would adopt this strategy?

    A   To reduce the overall risk of its organisation

    B   To free up management time within the organisation

    C   To enable growth if its current market is saturated

    D   To increase the number of synergies enjoyed by the organisation

120 NET Ltd owns a chain of factories which process iron ore into iron girders. They have recently purchased BLP – an iron ore mine in country H, which was one of their major suppliers for the previous year. NET have regularly changed suppliers in the past in order to obtain the lowest prices for iron ore. There are many similar iron ore mines in the world, though many of NET's rivals have also started purchasing mines.

Based on the above information, which of the following statements relating to NET's acquisition of BLP are correct? (Select ALL that apply).

    A   NET will enjoy guaranteed supply of iron ore, ensuring that its raw materials needs are met

    B   NET will have increased ability to differentiate its product in the market

    C   NET's acquisition of BLP will help it to avoid lock-out within its market

    D   NET will find it easier to source the lowest cost iron ore on the market

    E   NET is likely to enjoy improved economies of avoiding the market

121 UY is a manufacturer of motor vehicles. It has recently decided to start manufacturing motorbikes and scooters in an attempt to provide what UY's Managing Director referred to as 'a full range of transport solutions to our customers'.

Which ONE of the following types of diversification is UY undertaking?

    A   Forward vertical

    B   Backwards vertical

    C   Conglomerate

    D   Horizontal

MAKING STRATEGIC CHOICES – 15%

PORTFOLIO ANALYSIS

122 The following diagram shows the Boston Consulting Group (BCG) matrix.

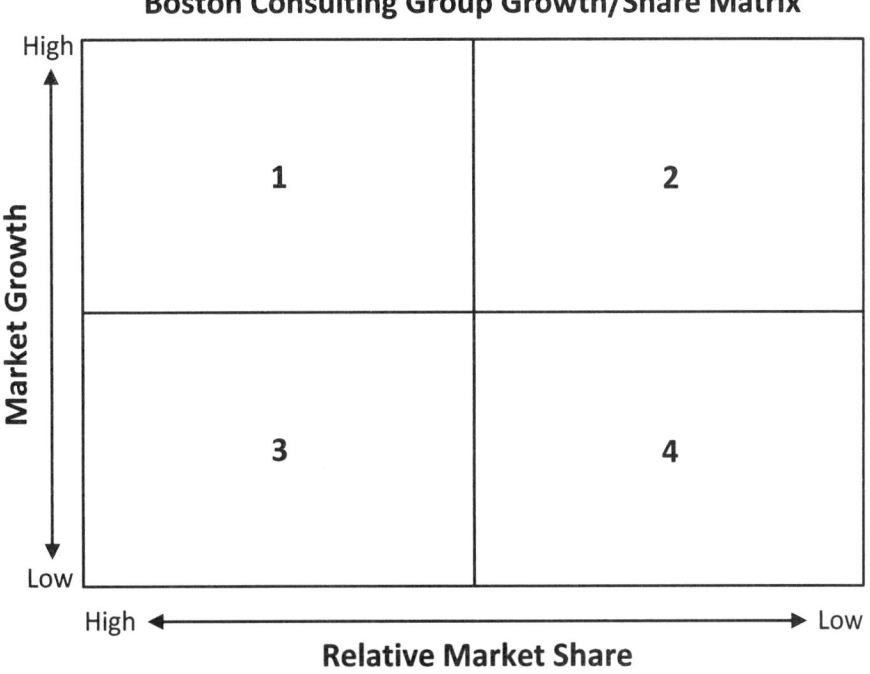

KDF plc has undertaken an analysis of one of its major products – JoyB – using the BCG matrix and has classified it as a star product.

Which ONE of the four quadrants on the above diagram would JoyB be included within?

A Quadrant 1

B Quadrant 2

C Quadrant 3

D Quadrant 4

123 JIH has decided to adopt a 'holding' strategy for several of its products.

Which TWO of the following classifications of product (according to the Boston Consulting Group matrix) would this strategy be most suitable for?

A Dog

B Star

C Cash cow

D Question mark

124 W is a multinational conglomerate, with four Strategic Business Units (SBUs). Data relating to those units, and the markets in which they are active, is shown below.

SBU	Market growth rate	Market share	Market share of largest rival
Alpha	High	4%	3%
Bravo	High	12%	40%
Charlie	Low	4%	15%
Delta	Negative	25%	8%

Analyse the product portfolio of W and classify each SBU, using the Boston Consulting Group (BCG) matrix.

	SBU		BCG matrix classification
A	Alpha	1	Dog
B	Bravo	2	Cash cow
C	Charlie	3	Star
D	Delta	4	Question mark

Identify which SBU relates to each BCG matrix classification by pairing the appropriate letter and number (e.g. A1, B2, etc).

125 SOH sells soap powder and other cleaning products. The company has decided to analyse its current portfolio of products using the Boston Consulting Group (BCG) matrix.

One of SOH's products is Darz – a powdered detergent. Darz was the market leader fifteen years ago, but has failed to keep pace with more modern products (such as gels) entering the cleaning market, which is now very mature. Darz is now the seventh highest selling detergent in the market and SOH thinks its market share is likely to decline further in the future.

Darz is still slightly profitable and, while relatively few consumers purchase it, many remember the brand name and SOH believes this supports the sale of other SOH products.

Which ONE of the following BCG strategies is most appropriate for SOH to adopt with regards to Darz?

A   Hold

B   Build

C   Harvest

D   Divest

126 TIH sells three products.

- ARC – this product is a market leader in the personal computer printer market, which is growing quickly.
- BUY – this is a sophisticated 3D printer. The market is high growth, but BUY only has a small share of the market.
- GUD – this is the fourth most popular printer in the office and commercial market. This market has been mature for many years.

V is a business consultant that has been hired by TIH. She has undertaken Boston Consulting Group (BCG) matrix analysis of TIH's portfolio and is very concerned.

Which ONE of the following statements relating to TIH's portfolio is correct?

A   TIH's products would all be placed in the same quadrant of the BCG matrix

B   TIH's products are all likely to enter decline at approximately the same time

C   TIH is likely to be having liquidity problems due to its current portfolio mix

D   TIH should consider divesting BUY due to its low market share

STRATEGY EVALUATION

127 GHA is a provider of training courses for surveyors. It is one of only three main organisations that provide this service in country K.

GHA is uncertain whether to grow by opening new training facilities across country K, or by acquiring one of its rivals.

Which THREE of the following are factors that would encourage GHA to choose organic growth rather than acquisition?

A   GHA is under pressure from major shareholders for rapid growth in sales

B   GHA has relatively low cash reserves and little access to additional finance

C   The government of country K has strict rules on monopolies and mergers

D   One of GHA's rivals may soon be acquired by a multinational training conglomerate with significant resources

E   GHA's rivals have significantly different corporate cultures to GHA itself

128 AAL plc, a skilled electronics manufacturing company, wishes to enter the market for the production and sale of communication satellites. However, the cost of creating production and launch facilities is significant, with no guarantee of eventual success. AAL has therefore approached OPO – a company based in the aviation industry – and suggested that the two companies collaborate on the creation of appropriate satellite production facilities, sharing expertise, as well as the risks and rewards, equally.

Which ONE of the following methods of joint development would be most appropriate for the collaboration between AAL and OPO?

A Licensing

B Joint venture

C Outsourcing

D Informal strategic alliance

129 QQH is a new chain of restaurants, which has two premises in the capital city of country H that have been open for two months. QQH is owned and solely managed by R, who has little experience running a business.

QQH has been successful in the capital city, so R wishes to grow the number of restaurants in the chain rapidly, but currently has little additional cash to invest, so he has decided to start selling QQH franchises in towns and cities across its home country. QQH has a very distinct style for its restaurants and R wants to ensure that this was replicated across all franchised premises.

How suitable would franchising be for QQH? (Choose ONE of the following options)

A VERY – it will help them achieve all of their strategic goals

B QUITE – while it would enable rapid growth it may be difficult to attract franchisees

C NOT VERY – it may be difficult to attract franchisees and ensure adequate controls

D NOT AT ALL – franchising would have no benefits and many risks for QQH

130 PPW manufactures refrigeration units. It has factories in country A which produce motor units, as well as other factories in country B which produce the refrigerator casing and other components. PPW then sends these goods to its facilities in its home country – country C, where they are assembled into the final product, which is sold to various countries around the world.

Which international growth strategy has PPW adopted?

A Multinational

B Overseas manufacture

C Transnational

D Exporting

131 BOQ is a charity which employs a large number of disabled staff members. It manufactures and sells mobility aids, such as crutches, and has the mission statement 'to support the citizens of country F who are in need.'

In the last two years, however, BOQ has seen a significant drop in the number of mobility aids it has sold as the market has become flooded with cheaper, imported products. This has led to BOQ posting significant losses.

At a recent meeting with the other trustees, the CEO of BOQ suggested that the charity should consider outsourcing much of BOQ's production overseas to ensure the charity continued to be able to afford to operate. He noted that staff were not heavily unionised and that the outsourcing process would not break any laws in country F.

The outsourcing strategy _____1_____ suitable.

The outsourcing strategy _____2_____ acceptable.

The outsourcing strategy _____3_____ feasible.

Use the options below to fill in the missing words in gaps 1, 2 and 3.

A   is

B   is not

132 CHA is an airline based in country V. It has a strong reputation for quality and caters to the premium end of the market, with a particular focus on business travel customers and wealthy holiday makers. To support this it offers excellent customer services (supported by large numbers of unionised staff), convenient flight schedules, comfortable airport lounges and a large amount of legroom on its aircraft.

Recently country V has suffered from a major recession, which has led to a significant fall in CHA's revenues and profitability. CHA has noted that many of its holiday maker customers have moved to cheaper, budget airlines. These airlines (of which there are many in country V) have low cost bases and this has allowed them to offer fares at far lower prices than CHA. However, they do not offer the same level of service and have no business class offering.

CHA has a small cash surplus and the new CEO of CHA has suggested that the company uses this to re-launch CHA as a budget airline. Many of the other members of the Board of Directors have reacted angrily to the suggestion, saying that the CEO clearly has no understanding of CHA's culture, or the extremely negative reaction the company's staff would have to the proposals.

Using the SAF framework developed by Johnson and Scholes, should CHA adopt the CEO's proposal? (Select ONE of the following options).

A   YES – the proposal is suitable, feasible and acceptable

B   YES – the proposal is suitable and feasible, but not acceptable

C   NO – the proposal is acceptable, but not suitable or feasible

D   NO – the proposal is not suitable, feasible or acceptable

SUBJECT E3 : STRATEGIC MANAGEMENT

133 JJJ plc is planning to undertake an evaluation of a particular strategy using the SAF model popularised by Johnson and Scholes.

Which ONE of the following strategic analysis models is JJJ most likely to use to help it decide whether the strategy is acceptable?

- A SWOT analysis
- B PEST analysis
- C Resource audit
- D Stakeholder mapping (Mendelow Matrix)

STRATEGIC CONTROL – 20%

PERFORMANCE MANAGEMENT SYSTEMS

134 Q is a local governmental organisation (council) for a town in country U. It has a large call centre to deal with queries and complaints from local residents and aims to 'help callers find the information they need'. Callers are asked to grade their satisfaction levels from 1 to 10 once they have completed their call, depending on how satisfied they were with their service. Currently, the higher the average grades given by callers across the year, the higher the bonus given to call centre staff. The call centre experiences a high volume of calls, with a number of calls going unanswered.

Q has recently decided to change the performance mix for its call centre staff. Staff will now be assessed on three separate measures: the number of calls taken by the centre in the period, the average speed with which the call is handled and the total number of complaints about call centre service received by Q. Each of these three measures will contribute equally to call centre staff bonuses.

Based on the above information, which TWO of the following statements relating to the proposed changes to performance measurement by Q are correct?

- A The new performance measurement mix may suggest to staff that the quality of assistance given to callers is no longer a high priority
- B The performance measurement mix should not be changed as this will disrupt the culture of Q's call centre staff
- C The new performance measurement mix measures may conflict with each other, causing confusion amongst call centre staff
- D The new performance measurement mix is inappropriate as it fails to include financial measures

135 K has a sum of money that she wishes to invest into WY plc. She has identified that WY's return on capital employed (ROCE) has fallen over the last year from 12% to 8%.

Which ONE of the following statements relating to WY's falling ROCE is correct?

A It may have been caused by falls in the level of equity within WY during the year

B It may have been caused by unusually large dividend payments during the year

C It may suggest that WY is a less attractive investment than it was last year

D It may indicate improved cost control within WY during the year

136 POG Ltd is a fashion design, manufacturing and retail company which is designing a new performance measurement mix for its employees. It currently only uses financial measures, but is considering including a number of non-financial measures into the mix.

Which of the following are factors that would encourage POG to include non-financial measures in its performance measurement mix? (Select ALL that apply)

A POG's wishes to keep the cost of measuring performance as low as possible

B POG's managers want to ensure that all measures are free from subjectivity

C The number of complaints relating to POG's product quality is rising

D Many of POG's staff have no understanding of POG's company finances

E POG wishes its performance measures to be consistent across all divisions

137 X is a mobile telecommunications company. It provides a network, through which calls can be routed, and enters into agreements with mobile telephone users. Some of the users buy call time, messages and data in advance ('pay and go'), while others pay a fixed amount each month in return for a package of calls, messages and data, with a limit set for each ('contract').

X is in the process of introducing The Balanced Scorecard, as a means of translating its mission into action. As part of this process, X has identified a number of objectives.

Match each objective to the appropriate perspective of its Balanced Scorecard (BS).

	BS Perspective		Objective
A	Financial perspective	1	Develop five new contract packages over the coming year
B	Learning and growth	2	Reduce total number of complaints received by 15%
C	Customer perspective	3	Grow revenues by 5% per annum
D	Internal business process	4	Reduce number of calls which fail due to network faults by 45%

Identify which objective relates to each BS perspective by pairing the appropriate letter and number (e.g. A1, B2, etc).

138 CRR offers tax planning and advice services to its customers through a chain of offices and is currently undertaking a Balanced Scorecard (BS) process within the business.

Identify which TWO of the following would be classified as 'internal business process' indicators within the BS framework.

- A The number of errors in client tax returns submitted by CRR
- B The average number of hours of training CRR staff underwent in the last year
- C The average time taken to calculate client tax liabilities
- D The amount of money invested in the development of a new online customer service

139 O is a charity that protects and maintains an area of forest which is home to a number of important animal and plant species. O is also responsible for maintaining safe paths for the many visitors to the forest.

Identify which ONE of the following would be an appropriate 'financial' indicator for O within the BS framework.

- A The change in O's return on capital employed for the year
- B O's operating profit margins for the year
- C O's investment in the development of new paths for visitors
- D The efficiency in the use of O's fund raising expenditure

140 Which THREE of the following are drawbacks of using the Balanced Scorecard (BS) model?

- A The BS does not provide a single view of performance which can lead to confusion
- B There is no clear link between the balanced scorecard and shareholder analysis
- C The BS mainly focuses on short-term measures, leading to long-term problems
- D The BS forces each division within an organisation to use identical indicators
- E Measures within the BS can conflict with each other, leading to confusion

141 Which ONE of the following would be classified as an external effectiveness measure within the Lynch and Cross performance pyramid?

- A Cycle time
- B Quality
- C Waste
- D Productivity

142 FFT runs a factory which manufactures speakers. It has identified that a major critical success factor in its market is the quality of the speaker.

Which level of the Lynch and Cross performance pyramid would this measure be included within?

- A Business units
- B Corporate vision
- C Departments and work centres
- D Business operating systems

OBJECTIVE TEST QUESTIONS : SECTION 1

143   Which THREE of the following are dimensions of the Fitzgerald and Moon building block model of performance measurement?

   A   Standards

   B   Profit

   C   Quality

   D   Rewards

   E   Flexibility

144   Q is considering the adoption of the Fitzgerald and Moon model to help him design a performance management system. From his studies, he is aware that the building block model stresses the need to set _____1_____ which are seen by employees as being both achievable and fair. The _____2_____ have to be chosen carefully to ensure that they are within the control of staff and of a sufficient size to motivate them.

   Use the options below to fill in the missing words in gaps 1 and 2.

   A   Dimensions

   B   Rewards

   C   Standards

145   VG is planning to introduce a new benchmarking procedure within its organisation, but is unsure which type of benchmarking would be most appropriate. It is aware that each type of benchmarking has certain drawbacks.

   VG has identified that _____1_____ benchmarking is often difficult to undertake as it is difficult to convince the other party to share information about their operations.

   _____2_____ benchmarking is unlikely to suggest any truly innovative solutions and is typically only useful where the organisation feels that conformity of service is crucial to its operations.

   Finally, _____3_____ benchmarking often fails to provide data on the benchmarking company's core functions as it requires the organisation to benchmark itself against an organisation in a different industry.

   Use the options below to fill in the missing words in gaps 1, 2 and 3.

   A   Process

   B   Internal

   C   Competitive

SUBJECT E3 : STRATEGIC MANAGEMENT

146 KV operates a van rental company through a chain of around 35 stores. It has received a number of complaints from customers about the service they have received. KV's investigation has revealed that different stores are offering radically different levels of service to customers, with many stores providing excellent customer service and others performing poorly.

KV is the current market leader in the van rental market, with a market share which is significantly ahead of its nearest rival. KV's managers are still keen to ensure their market share does not fall and have decided to undertake a benchmarking process to help the business standardise the level of service it offers to customers across its business.

Which ONE of the following types of benchmarking would be most appropriate for KV to adopt?

- A Process
- B Strategic
- C Competitive
- D Internal

147 HU plc is a multinational company that is considering a new project. While the project is still in the planning stage, HU is keen to ensure that the project is run in a way which is consistent with a shareholder value analysis (SVA) approach.

Which TWO of the following are consistent with an SVA approach?

- A Adjusting the reported profit figures for the project to remove the effect of GAAP
- B Designing strategies to maximise the useful life of the project
- C Examining ways of reducing or spreading out the project's initial asset investment
- D Including the valuation of the project's intangible assets, such as brand and goodwill

148 You have recently been talking to a colleague about the use of Triple Bottom Line reporting in your organisation. Your colleague made the following statement:

'Triple bottom line reporting would involve us measuring our organisation's profit, as well as our impact on people and the planet. Measuring all of these things is very straightforward for most businesses. It could be a useful way for our business to encourage staff to make efficiency cost savings and could even help us attract ethically aware staff and customers.'

Which ONE of the following statements best describes your colleague's understanding of Triple Bottom Line (TBL) reporting?

- A EXCELLENT – there she has shown a total understanding of TBL reporting
- B GOOD – there is only one mistake in what she has told you about TBL reporting
- C POOR – there are two mistakes in what she has told you about TBL reporting
- D VERY POOR – there are more than two mistakes in what she has told you about TBL reporting

149 OPO has recently decided to create a new staff performance measurement system. Previously OPO's staff were only paid a basic salary regardless of performance. The new system will involve monitoring a range of employee performance issues, such as total work hours, errors made by each employee and absenteeism. This will form the basis of a bonus that each employee can earn each year.

OPO's Human Resource Manager (HRM) has suggested that before OPO launches its new system, it should be discussed with employees and feedback sought.

Which of the following would be benefits to OPO of following the HRM's suggestion? (Select ALL that apply).

- A Improved understanding of what the employees need to do to meet their targets
- B OPO can ensure that targets are seen as achievable by its staff
- C Reduced chance that OPO staff will behave unethically to achieve the new targets
- D Increased employee buy-in to the new system, improving motivation

150 J is a manager at a firm of surveyors. Currently, his staff perform an average of 5 house surveys per day and this has left the business with a sizeable backlog of surveys to undertake. J wishes to raise this to 8 per day. While he is not offering staff a bonus for achieving this new level of performance, he is sure that as it will benefit the business they will happily accept the new targets.

J has announced the new targets to his staff, who were surprised as J had not previously consulted them about this issue, though most employees stated privately that they could reach the new targets if they hurried through each of their surveys.

Which TWO of the following problems is J most likely to face with the stretch targets he has set?

- A Staff see the target as unachievable and are demotivated by them
- B The new targets lead to sub-optimal behaviour by staff
- C Staff will feel no motivation to work towards the stretch target
- D Stretch targets are being set for staff in an area that will not benefit the business

151 The International Integrated Reporting Council (IIRC) has produced an Integrated Reporting Framework which sets out seven guiding principles that have to be considered when preparing an integrated report.

Which of the following is contained within the seven guiding principles? Select ALL that apply.

- A Strategic focus and future orientation
- B Connectivity of information
- C Stakeholder relationships
- D Conciseness
- E Materiality

152 The Integrated Reporting Framework emphasises the relationships between what it identifies as the 'six capitals'.

Which ONE of the following is NOT contained within the six capitals?

A   Institutional

B   Natural

C   Manufactured

D   Intellectual

CHANGE MANAGEMENT

153 PI Ltd operates a chain of tanning shops across country F.

PI has recently undertaken a detailed analysis of external triggers for change. It has identified the following:

A   Increased government health and safety legislation relating to tanning stores

B   Recession within country F leading to a fall in consumer disposable income

C   TYS, a new tanning company, is offering tanning to customers at heavy discounts

D   WAM – suppliers of sun beds in country F has closed, leaving only one company offering the tanning beds that PI uses in its stores

E   Tanning has started to be seen as unfashionable by consumers in country F

For each of the above triggers, identify whether they are indirect or direct triggers by placing the appropriate letters into the table below.

Indirect triggers	Direct triggers

154 The following diagram shows Balogun Hope Hailey's model of organisation change.

Extent of change

	Transformation	Realignment
Incremental	1	2
Bing Bang	3	4

Speed of change

X has identified that the change occurring within her organisation would be classified as 'adaptation'.

Which ONE of the four quadrants on the above diagram would X's change be placed within?

A   Quadrant 1

B   Quadrant 2

C   Quadrant 3

D   Quadrant 4

155 MMM GmbH is a large multi-national conglomerate based in Europe which manufactures tinned goods. It has recently been acquired by OOO plc, a UK based food manufacturer.

While the two organisations have fundamentally different cultures and working practices, OOO management are determined that MMM as an organisation is aligned with OOO quickly and that all managerial practices conform to the OOO way of doing things.

Select which ONE of the following classifications of change MMM's employees are most likely to believe this change process represents.

A   Evolution

B   Adaption

C   Revolution

D   Reconstruction

SUBJECT E3 : STRATEGIC MANAGEMENT

156 AVV is a charity which provides education for underprivileged children in country V. A recent change in government has led to new legislation which has provided state funded education for all underprivileged children. The charity has therefore had to rapidly change its core mission to *'helping provide education for underprivileged children throughout the world'*. This has meant that AVV's management have had to consider drastically new ways of spending the money they raise to support education in countries that they currently have little familiarity with – although AVV's fundraising efforts have required little change.

Which of the following statements regarding the change occurring in AVV are correct? Select ALL that apply.

- A   Different stakeholders within AVV may perceive the change as being either a transformation or a realignment
- B   The change in legislation is an example of an indirect change trigger for AVV
- C   AVV's recent shift in strategy is an example of 'incremental' organisational change
- D   AVV's recent could be considered an example of 'evolution' as the change has been a forced reaction to changes in the charity's environment

157 Which THREE of the following are elements of an organisation's cultural web?

- A   Organisational structure
- B   Organisational systems
- C   Routines and rituals
- D   Management style
- E   Organisational paradigm

158 Hexagon Ltd is a small manufacturing company that makes toys. Mr Who established the company over a hundred years ago. Mr Who's son now runs the company. The manufacturing site is in the heart of the city centre and still houses some of the original machines used to make toys many years ago. Employees regularly talk about the need for work to be done 'how it's always been done.'

Select the ONE element of Hexagon's cultural web would best describe the above.

- A   Power structure
- B   Control systems
- C   Stories and myths
- D   Organisational structure

159 McKinsey's 7S model identifies a number of factors of corporate culture. These include:

- A   Staff
- B   Skills
- C   Structure
- D   Shared values
- E   Strategy
- F   Styles
- G   Systems

For each of the above factors, identify whether they are 'hard' or 'soft' factors by placing the appropriate letters into the table below.

Hard	Soft

160 CVV plc's management adopts an authoritarian approach and simply tell staff what they want them to do. CVV's management do not involve staff in their decision making process.

Which ONE of the following factors from McKinsey's 7S model of corporate culture is being described above?

- A   Structure
- B   Shared values
- C   Staff
- D   Style

161 AXX plc operates a chain of supermarkets which is currently undergoing a period of rapid change. AXX has been successful for many years, in spite of significant rivalry within its industry. It has pursued a differentiation strategy by having large numbers of well trained staff in store to help customers with their shopping needs. Staff pride themselves on the level of service they offer and bonuses are based on the feedback they receive from customers. Staff are typically included in all major management decisions.

Recently, AXX has started losing market share to a new rival, ZOZ. ZOZ is a chain of discount supermarkets that charge low prices for a similar range of products to AXX. ZOZ's arrival in the market has coincided with a recession in AXX's major markets, which has left consumers with less disposable income.

In the last twelve months, AXX's sales have fallen by twenty percent and it is on course to make its first ever loss in the next trading year. AXX has therefore hired a new CEO who previously operated a budget airline. He has immediately started cost-cutting exercises (with no staff consultation), including significant redundancies and the removal of bonus schemes. He has publically dismissed employee criticism of his proposals as 'stupidity'.

While staff are not heavily unionised, they have close working relationships with each other in most stores, often building friendships outside of the workplace.

Which of the following factors are likely to be 'social' factors that will lead to resistance to these changes by AXX employees? (Select ALL that apply)

A Fear of unemployment

B Loss of interaction with current staff members

C Lack of consultation by new CEO

D Implied criticism of current working methods

E Dislike of the new CEO

162 QQS is a business that sells gravel and stone. It has recently announced the launch of a new purchasing system which it has publically stated 'will help our business to reduce its inventory management costs by fifteen percent per annum'.

Employees in the purchasing department of QQS have stated their opposition to the introduction of the new system, as they are convinced that the cost savings will be through job losses within the department.

In fact, QQS is planning to make the savings through reduced inventory holding costs thanks to the new system allowing them to reduce the amount of inventory held at any given time. However, QQS's management have yet to explain this to staff.

According to Kotter and Schlesinger, which ONE of the following four reasons for resistance best explains the reaction of QQS's purchasing department staff?

A Misunderstanding

B Parochial self-interest

C Low tolerance to change

D Different assessments of the situation

163 Delaware Ltd is about to go through a significant restructuring. The strategic change involves moving from a decentralised to a centralised structure. This will help Delaware avoid duplication of support activities and lower its costs.

The management have held the first staff briefing in which they went to great lengths to explain that the change was necessary to equip the company to face future competitive challenges.

Which ONE stage of Lewin's three-stage model of change are Delaware currently within?

A   Unfreeze

B   Refreeze

C   Change

D   Reinforcement

164 XA is a vehicle rental company. The company operates 35 vehicle rental depots – each with its own staff and fleet of vehicles. Staff are very focused on providing well-maintained, clean vehicles for rental. Many staff have worked for XA for many years and most started their career as vehicle technicians.

In recent years, XA been losing market share. In response to this, the business has developed a new mission statement:

'XA aims to be the first choice vehicle rental company, by providing well-maintained vehicles at an affordable price, and excellent customer service.'

This is the first new mission produced by XA in many years and differs from the previous mission statement, in that it includes the phrase 'and excellent customer service'.

In order to improve customer service levels, The Marketing Director (MD) has told the Marketing Manager (J) that she must change the marketing approach from 'transactions marketing' to 'relationship marketing'. J is concerned about overcoming resistance to this change, as she has never implemented a major change programme.

J has analysed the various factors that might influence the success of the proposed change, using Lewin's Forcefield model. These factors are:

A   The existing product-oriented culture

B   The length of service by staff

C   The Marketing Director

D   The new mission statement

E   Staff background in vehicle maintenance

F   J's competencies with relationship marketing

G   Loss of market share

For each of the above factors, identify whether they are 'driving' or 'restraining' factors in Lewin's Forcefield model by placing the appropriate letters into the table below.

Driving	Restraining

165 KK is implementing a major new IT system across its entire operations and is using Lewin's three-stage model to help it control the process.

Which TWO of the following activities would be classified within Lewin's three-stage model as 'refreezing'?

- A Setting up new reporting relationships for staff using the new system
- B Staff training in use of the new system
- C Promotion of staff who support the new system
- D Publicity of 'success stories' relating to successful use of the new system

166 S runs three flower shops. She has recently found that demand for her products has declined and this has led to a fall in profits.

Which ONE of the following actions by S would be consistent with a 'Theory E' approach, as described by Beer and Nohria?

- A Undertaking additional marketing training to help her improve her ability to attract customers
- B Reduce the number of staff working in each shop and use this cost saving to allow S to cut her selling prices
- C Discussing the problem with her staff and brainstorming new ideas for the business
- D Look for ways to improve customer service within the stores to improve customer retention

167 HO is an investment bank in country A. Its employees are highly skilled and work long hours, rarely taking holidays or time for other activities. In return, HO pays very high wages – with annual bonuses that can be equal to the employee's annual basic pay. HO's staff are among the highest paid workers in country A and lead lavish lifestyles. They are seen as a core competence by the bank's management and would be hard to replace.

HO has decided to implement stricter controls on employee investment activities after a number of its rivals have been heavily fined for illegal investment deals – one of HO's rivals was forced into liquidation by the size of its fine. HO has decided to launch a new computer system that will restrict its employees from undertaking unauthorised deals.

HO's staff have reacted angrily to this, saying that they do not see the need for a new IT system and that HO's suggestion indicates that the management do not trust them.

Which ONE of the following activities would be the best way for the organisation to reduce resistance from its employees to the new system?

A Offering increased pay and rewards to staff who adopt the new system

B Offering detailed training for staff on the use of the new system, including ongoing technical support and assistance

C Increased communication and explanation that the new system is in employees' best interests

D Exercise of authority by HO management - simply implement the system regardless of employee resistance

168 LJH plc is a large multi-national based in Europe which has just appointed a new CEO. The new CEO has some very exciting ideas about the future direction for LJH. All her ideas will require careful, thoughtful change management. She has therefore decided to appoint herself as a change leader.

Select which THREE of the following steps would be incorporated in the change leader's role?

A Establish a sense of urgency

B Appoint a new Board of Directors

C Communicate a vision

D Incorporate changes into culture

E Instigate voluntary redundancies where necessary

F Co-opt staff into accepting the change

169 G has recently started work as the new CEO of V plc – a company which makes and sells computer monitors. G is aware that, while V has the largest market share of the global computer monitor market, it has old-fashioned production techniques which mean it has one of the lowest operating margins in its industry.

G therefore decided to implement a major shift in the organisation's operations. She created a detailed plan known as 'V plc – the way forward' and spent a great deal of time communicating this to staff. She also created a series of interim goals which she thinks will be easy for the company to reach, giving employees motivation to implement the ongoing changes required.

Ultimately, even though several interim goals were met, G failed to fully implement her vision. G stated that this was because even though senior management had agreed to help her implement the plans, they thought that V's position as market leader meant that it did not need really need to make internal improvements.

According to Kotter's model, which of the 8 steps of change leadership had G failed to meet?

- A Developing a change vision
- B Creating a guiding coalition
- C Generating short-term wins
- D Establishing a sense of urgency

170 FDZ is experiencing a crisis in its operations, as one of its major product lines has been banned by law in its largest market. FDZ's directors have proposed that the company forms a team of senior employees from across its various departments to brainstorm ideas for how to radically change the product to enable it to meet the new legislation. FDZ feels that if this is not done within the next four weeks, long-term damage will be done to the company's reputation in the market.

Which TWO of the following statements about teams would FDZ need to consider before proceeding?

- A The use of a team could slow FDZ's decision-making down, which the company cannot afford
- B The use of a team would likely reduce the level of communication between the different departments within FDZ
- C Group pressure to conform could lead to team members agreeing to amendments to FDZ's product that they do not feel are suitable
- D There will be reduced ability for the team's work to be reviewed and controlled, meaning FDZ should consider having an individual make the relevant product decisions

171 Which ONE of the following is a leadership style within Kotter and Schlesinger's model?

- A Autocratic
- B Coercive
- C Competitive
- D Retrenchment

OBJECTIVE TEST QUESTIONS : SECTION 1

172 HRH sells memorabilia and ornaments to tourist shops across country M. It makes strong profits each year, but is considering the launch of a new production system that will reduce its overheads and increase margins. It will also allow HRH to make around 15% of its workforce redundant.

HRH's CEO has made a number of different suggestions as to how staff could be managed, but is unsure which of Kotter and Schlesinger's leadership styles each one relates to.

Consider the following lists of leadership styles and the approaches suggested by the CEO.

	Leadership style		CEO suggestion
A	Facilitation and support	1	Discuss the new system with HRH employees and see if they have any useful ideas about how to minimise the impact of the proposal on workers.
B	Education and communication	2	Give staff who are to be made redundant time off and help them find other jobs.
C	Manipulation and co-optation	3	Tell staff that the company is experiencing financial difficulties and that the new system will ensure its survival.
D	Participation	4	Explain the benefits that the proposed change will have to the organisation in an attempt to reduce staff resistance.

Identify which leadership style correlates to each of the CEO's suggestions by pairing the appropriate letter and number (e.g. A1, B2, etc).

173 G Ltd has a small workforce that is highly skilled and motivated. G feels that many of its staff members would be difficult for the company to replace and it therefore needs to maintain a strong, ongoing relationship with them.

G is about to implement a major series of change and is concerned about employee resistance. The changes will involve twenty redundancies, which is the minimum that G feels will enable the company to avoid insolvency. The redundancies will need to be made over the next eighteen months.

Which ONE Kotter and Schlesinger leadership style would be most appropriate for G to adopt?

A Power/coercion

B Negotiation

C Manipulation and co-optation

D Education and communication

174 J has been hired as a change agent by the directors of BB plc.

Which the following roles would J undertake as a change agent? (Select all that apply)

- A Make the final decision on which change strategy to adopt
- B Document the learning process and share this information
- C Implement the change process
- D Define the problems and its causes
- E Suggest solutions and select appropriate courses of action

175 Which THREE of the following are included within Kanter's 'power skills of change agents' model?

- A Self-confidence tempered with humility
- B State-of-the-art knowledge of the required change
- C Fresh perspective
- D Ability to work independently
- E Willingness to stake personal rewards on results

176 Consider the following statements:

- A The provider acts as an ongoing role model
- B Offers wide-ranging, practical advice and support
- C Is usually undertaken for a specific, defined period
- D Tends to focus on specific skills and goals
- E More likely to cover both technical and non-technical areas

For each of the above factors, identify whether they are relate to executive mentoring or coaching by placing the appropriate letters into the table below.

Executive mentoring	Executive coaching

OBJECTIVE TEST QUESTIONS : SECTION 1

177 HAP plc manufactures bicycles. Until recently it has adopted a differentiation strategy, offering high quality bicycles which HAP sells at a high profit margin.

In recent years, HAP has entered a period of decline thanks to the market becoming flooded with cheaper, high quality bicycles from abroad, where labour costs are lower.

HAP has therefore decided to adjust its strategy and adopt a focus approach, targeting its bicycles towards professional athletes. This will allow HAP to continue earning high margins, though the size of its potential market will likely fall.

Which ONE of the following strategies to manage decline has HAP adopted?

A   Retrenchment

B   Liquidation

C   Turnaround

D   Divestment

178 P is undergoing a major change within its operations in an attempt to cut costs and return the business to profitability. G is currently employed as a strategic management accountant within P.

As a professional accountant, which of the following change strategies is inconsistent with G's code of professional ethics?

A   Redundancies in all sectors of the business

B   Cutting staff working hours

C   Adopting a coercive management style

D   Manipulation of information provided to staff

179 Kanter suggested that managers within change-adept organisations have a number of key skills.

U is a manager in X Ltd, which has recently launched a new IT system for its staff. U was asked to lead the launch of the system and immediately set up a series of interim goals, which staff would be rewarded for as soon as they were reached.

Which ONE of Kanter's change leadership skills is U demonstrating?

A   Building coalitions

B   Making everyone a hero

C   Communicating a compelling aspiration

D   Learning to persevere

180 **Which TWO of the following statements is consistent with Peter's 'Thriving on Chaos' theory?**

A   Incremental change is the enemy of true innovation

B   Excellent firms believe in constant improvement and change

C   Change should always be implemented as rapidly as possible

D   Management need to transfer ownership to the work team

DIGITAL STRATEGY – 15%

DIGITAL TECHNOLOGIES

181 F has recently started gathering extremely large volumes of information about his customers. His main concern is that his customers' details are changing rapidly and he is uncertain how to prevent his data becoming out of date.

Which ONE aspect of Gartner's 4Vs model is F having difficulties with?

- A Veracity
- B Velocity
- C Volume
- D Variety

182 Which THREE of the following are typical problems that organisations may face when dealing with Big Data?

- A The increasing use of electronic devices within society at large
- B A lack of skills in the labour pool relating to the handling of Big Data
- C Legal and privacy issues if data is held about individuals
- D Measurement of metrics that have no use to the organisation
- E Inability to monitor information from social media sites

183 Ms Cole is CEO of Starfish, a group of six technology companies that recently merged to form a complete 'ecosystem'.

In a presentation to the Senior Management team of Starfish, Ms Cole gave an inspirational and passionate argument why digitalisation is the only way for Starfish to succeed. She called of the Senior Management team to take this message to their staff, and asked for the support of everyone in gaining the commitment of the whole Group.

In order to successfully manage the 'move to digital', the executive leadership team must demonstrate a number of abilities.

Analyse the above information and identify which ONE of those abilities is being demonstrated by Ms Cole.

- A Establishing a Strategic Direction
- B Collaboration
- C Inspirational Leadership
- D Business Judgement

OBJECTIVE TEST QUESTIONS : SECTION 1

184 MidLife is a specialist insurance company, targeting customers aged between 30 and 60 years old.

MidLife is transferring all of its computing to a 'virtual server' on the Internet. This will allow for far greater storage capacity, and staff will be able to access and process data from any location with Wi-Fi or a mobile signal using a laptop or cellphone.

Identify which ONE of the following MidLife is adopting.

A   Cloud storage

B   Big Data analytics

C   Cloud and mobile computing

D   Bots

185 Rayner is a large manufacturer of recipe dishes (food products that can be kept refrigerated, then cooked in an oven or microwave). Rayner's supply chain is very complex, as it buys ingredients from hundreds of suppliers in about twenty countries.

Rayner has invested in a 'bot', which pays supplier invoices without any human intervention. As a result, fewer suppliers are complaining about late payment, and Rayner has significantly reduced its processing costs.

Identify which ONE of the following approaches Rayner is using.

A   Process automation

B   Process re-engineering

C   Process innovation

D   Process reduction

186 101FM is a digital radio station. Launched in 2018, 101FM has already gained substantial audiences.

Until a few years ago, the country in which 101FM is based insisted on radio stations obtaining a license to operate. Getting a license was bureaucratic and time-consuming. As a result, very few new radio stations were formed. In addition, the State owned a large broadcasting company, which provided a range of different stations each catering for different tastes. This made gaining an audience difficult, and many new stations failed as they could not gain enough listeners to reach break-even point. However, it made promoting music relatively cheap, as record companies needed only to persuade a few stations to play their artists' output.

Prior to the growth of the Internet, providing radio services required huge investments in infrastructure. Radio stations needed expensive studio facilities and broadcast equipment including transmitters and relay stations. Now, a digital (via the Internet and 'broadcast from Internet') station can be set up at relatively low cost. Presenters can create shows at home, playing music streamed from the Internet. The broadcast processes have been automated by means of apps which can be installed on any mobile device. These provide presenters with all the functionality of a radio studio, without the need for any hardware.

Internet-only stations do not need a license. 'Broadcast from Internet' stations can have their output transmitted via 'Digital Audio Broadcast' (DAB) by broadcast companies. This allows radio stations to share the cost of licenses and transmission costs, vastly reducing their fixed costs.

As a result, the country in which 101FM is based now has over a thousand radio stations, compared with fewer than a hundred only ten years ago.

Analyse the above information and identify which of the following effects the development of digital broadcasting and the subsequent growth of stations like 101FM has had on the music radio ecosystem. Select ALL that apply.

A   Barriers to entry have fallen, thus increasing the Threat of New Entrants

B   The Bargaining Power of Customers has increased, due to a much wider choice of stations

C   The Bargaining Power of Suppliers has increased, as musicians and bands now have to promote their music to a much larger number of radio stations

D   Rivalry has increased, as low-cost operators have entered the industry

E   Digital radio is no longer perceived as a 'Substitute' to terrestrial radio

187   Stormy is an independent weather forecaster for sailors. Users subscribe to an app, and receive detailed weather forecasts to allow them to prepare for competitive or leisure sailing activities.

Stormy's app works in the following way:

1   The algorithm behind the app receives a wide range of data from public weather stations, and compares this to a large database of historic weather patterns. The app then predicts local weather based on what happened in the past.

2   The app then monitors the actual weather, as it evolves, and receives 'credits' based on the accuracy of its forecasts.

3   The app then learns how to improve its forecasts, and modifies its future forecasts.

Analyse the above information and identify what type of machine learning is being used by Stormy.

A   Supervised learning

B   Unsupervised learning

C   Reinforcement learning

D   Organisational learning

188 Cimaron is a biotechnology company. It performs chemical analysis on millions of chemical compounds, using sophisticated analytics software to predict and model the likely effects of each on the human body.

At the end of a processing run, based on one 'family' of chemical compounds, the Cimaron software outputs details of only those compounds which it determines may be potential new drug discoveries. This determination uses a series of rules, which can be re-written by the software itself, to locate those compounds with the highest potential.

Discovery Analysts then examine the output data, using an application which allows them to see an Augmented Reality (AR) view of the human body, with the relevant data items 'pinned' to the appropriate part of the body. In this way, the Analysts can more easily understand the findings of the software and make a more reasoned decision whether to pass the potential drug discovery forward for further analysis.

Analyse the above information and identify which ONE of the following techniques is employed in the application being used by Cimaron's Discovery Analysts.

A   Big Data analytics

B   Data visualization

C   Artificial Intelligence (AI)

D   Blockchain

189 Firesmoke is an environmental protection organisation. It works with government bodies and commercial organisations to prevent and detect fire in countryside environments such as forests and moorland.

Firesmoke supplies smoke and heat sensors to its clients, which they 'seed' (often by dropping them from aircraft) over a very wide area. These sensors collect data about their environment, which is uploaded to the Internet. There, the data is aggregated with other data from multiple sources such as satellites and social media posts, and subjected to powerful algorithms which identify anomalies likely to be indicative of fire.

Firesmoke also provides clients with drones (autonomous aerial vehicles) which fly above the area being controlled. The drones collect video and infra-red data, which is added to the main data-set. Smoke is easy to see but can be due to campfires or barbecues. The algorithm is able to filter out this 'noise' and identify fires in their early stage.

It is sometimes necessary for Firesmoke's clients to engage government agencies or private organisations to 'fight' fires. These sub-contractors are provided with an app (supplied by Firesmoke) which overlays data points on video or live camera footage. This allows the user to 'see' data such as temperature or particulate matter when viewing a large area from a plane or vehicle. The video and data can be viewed on a laptop, smartphone or headset.

Analyse the above information and identify which of the following technologies are being used by Firesmoke. Select ALL that apply.

A   Internet of Things

B   Augmented Reality

C   Virtual Reality

D   Big Data analytics

E   Cloud and mobile

SUBJECT E3 : STRATEGIC MANAGEMENT

ELEMENTS OF DIGITAL STRATEGY

190 Mattiel is an online retail platform, specialising in Business-to-Business (B2B) supplies and services.

The Mattiel platform allows business buyers to join together to increase their bargaining power. Business sellers then 'bid' to satisfy the aggregated order. Mattiel takes a fee of 1% of each transaction.

According to the Digital Transformation of Industries Initiative (DTI) of the World Economic Forum, there are nine 'revenue models' available to disruptors.

Analyse the above information and identify which ONE of those models is being pursued by Mattiel.

- A Transaction
- B Licensing
- C Commission
- D Trading

191 Abong is a wholesaler of business commodities such as metals, plastics and basic components.

In this traditionally low-margin business, Abong has managed to make significant profits. Using sophisticated Big Data analytics software, Abong can buy commodities when they are relatively cheap and easy to obtain, then sell them when demand exceeds supply. Very little of Abong's inventory ever reaches them, as it is delivered straight from their supplier to their customer.

According to the Digital Transformation of Industries Initiative (DTI) of the World Economic Forum, there are nine 'revenue models' available to disruptors.

Analyse the above information and identify which ONE of those models is being pursued by Abong.

- A Transaction
- B Licensing
- C Commission
- D Trading

OBJECTIVE TEST QUESTIONS : SECTION 1

192 Bowie is a multinational engineering company. It was formed in 1953 and became a world leader in the manufacture of business automation equipment which, in those days, was mainly conveyor systems and production machinery. In the 1980s Bowie moved gradually into production robotics.

By 2010, Bowie was struggling. Other manufacturers had improved their products and those based in low-wage economies were able to under-cut Bowie on price.

In 2011, Bowie launched its Industrial Internet initiative to move toward an outcomes-based business model focused on big data and analytics. Digitally enabled and outcomes-based approaches helped Bowie generate more than $800 million in incremental income in 2013. In 2015, Bowie made the next step, with dramatic changes to its strategy and operations, with the creation of Bowie Digital. This move has helped Bowie bring together all the digital capabilities from across the company into one organisation with a bold ambition to grow software and analytics enterprise from $6 billion in 2015 to become a top 10 software company by 2020.

Research at the World Economic Forum on "Digital Transformation of Industries" suggests that companies need to adopt one of (or a combination of) build, buy, partner, invest and incubate/accelerate if they wish to identify, develop and launch new business ventures.

Identify which ONE of these is being pursued by Bowie.

A   Buy

B   Build

C   Invest

D   Partner

193 Crosby is a vineyard in southern England. It grows three varieties of grape on a site of several hectares. When the grapes are ripe, Crosby employs casuals labour to pick them. The grapes are then taken to a local town, where they are pressed into grape juice by Nash. Nash receives a few from Crosby, for this work.

The grape juice is then sent, by road tanker, to a winery about 50 km away. The winery is owned by the Stills Group, a national producer of wine, beer and cider. There, Crosby's grape juice is turned into wine by fermentation, filtering and bottling. This process takes several months, and Crosby pays two fees to Stills – one when the grape juice goes into fermentation, and a further one to release the bottled wine from storage. This latter fee varies, according to the alcohol content of the wine, as Stills must pay excise duty (tax), to the government, which is assessed on the basis of 'alcohol by volume'. When the wine is bottled, it is returned to Crosby. Crosby then stores the wine, decides when it is ready for consumption, and offers it for sale to wine brokers or retailers.

As the above relationships between Crosby, Nash and Stills have developed over many years, Crosby is now able to sell its wine at quite a high price. However, Crosby also has a considerable sum tied up in inventory.

Crosby has approached Nash and Stills to propose a new business model. A new company (CS&N) will be formed, owned 50% by Crosby and 25% each by Nash and Stills. CS&N will, in future, buy grapes from Crosby and other local vineyards. It will hold all the inventory, at each stage of the process, and will sell the finished wine. Nash will press the grapes at no cost to CS&N. Stills will turn the resulting juice into wine, again 'free of charge'. Crosby will sell the wine. Any profits made by CS&N will be shared by its owners.

SUBJECT E3 : STRATEGIC MANAGEMENT

Analyse the above information and identify which ONE of the following methods Crosby is planning to use, to change the way its ecosystem operates.

A   Joint Venture

B   Strategic Alliance

C   Licensing

D   Franchising

194   Jimmy James is CEO of Beastie Group, a major distributor of frozen and chilled foods.

Mr James is preparing a presentation on 'The Digital Revolution', which he plans to deliver to the Board of Beastie when it next meets. He is a little unsure of the difference between 'technology drivers' (those factors that have led to the revolution) and 'changing needs' (the new requirements of customers). He has asked you for your help.

Which of the following are technology trends driving the 'digital revolution', as mentioned by Mr James? Select ALL that apply.

A   Connected devices

B   Global accessibility

C   Contextual interactions

D   Transparency

E   Mobile and internet penetration

195   The Board of Sleaford, a large financial services Group, is having a 'strategy away-day'.

In this morning's brainstorming session, the Board developed the following list of 'digital trends'. This afternoon, the Board needs to make sense of them, and distinguish between those that are driving digitalisation in their industry, and those that are being developed as a response to those drivers. The list is:

1   Users searching for insurance products like to see feedback from other customers.

2   Banks are making extensive use of Big Data analytics and Cloud Storage.

3   Credit card customers seem to invest time and energy into finding exactly the 'right' product for them.

4   Online banking products from Sleaford's rivals allow users to 'speak' to their banking app, using normal speech.

5   In its African and Asian markets, Sleaford notices more customers moving from rural to urban locations.

Which of the factors identified are trends driving the 'digital revolution'? Select ALL that apply.

A   Peer review

B   Data analytics and the cloud

C   Self-service

D   User interfaces

E   Increasing urbanisation

OBJECTIVE TEST QUESTIONS : **SECTION 1**

196 Racing Green is a fashion brand, supplying fashion sportswear to multiples and independent retailers. Racing Green also has a sophisticated e-commerce platform, using a 'personal shopper' bot to advise customers based on previous purchases and fashion trends.

As part of its new strategy, Racing Green will fundamentally change the way its garments are produced for online customers. The personal shopper bot will be allowed to recommend combinations of garment, size and colour that Racing green's manufacturing system is capable of making, but which have never been made before. Customers will also be able to control logo size and placement, though they will not be able to specify garments without the company logo.

This will allow online customers to buy garments that are unique to them, and fit with their preferred style and colour palette.

Analyse the above information and select which ONE of the following is being used by Racing Green.

- A Design thinking
- B Experiential pilots
- C Prototyping
- D Brand atomization

197 Chic is an online dating site. Users complete a registration process, pay a monthly fee, and create a profile with photographs. After their profile is approved by Chic, a user can search the profiles of other registered users. Having been operational for twelve months, the management team of Chic has decided that it is time to start setting performance targets to monitor the growth of the business.

Digital traction is a combination of metrics in 3 areas: Scale, Active Usage, and Engagement.

Align the following by matching each type of metric with the relevant measure for Chic.

A	Scale	1	The number of likes and messages
B	Active usage	2	The number of repeat users
C	Engagement	3	The number of registered users

SUBJECT E3 : STRATEGIC MANAGEMENT

198 Stereolab is a music streaming site. It allows users, on payment of a small monthly subscription of $10, to stream any pieces of music they choose from the hundreds of thousands available. Users cannot download the music, so they must have Internet connectivity to use the service.

In the first three months (90 days) of this financial year, Stereolab produced the following performance data:

- At the beginning of the period, Stereolab had 1.35 million registered users, of whom 1.28 million had an active subscription (so were allowed to actually stream music). By the end of the period, this had grown to 1.44 million who were registered and 1.38 million of those were active and paid-up.
- The total marketing spend for the period was $32 million.
- A typical subscriber remains active for five years.

Analyse the above information and select which of the following statements are true for Stereolab. Select ALL that apply.

A The average 'Cost to Acquire a Customer' (CAC) was about $22 for the period

B Growth in registrations was approximately 2.2% per month

C The 'months to recover CAC' is about 36

D Active usage was 95.8% at the end of the period

E The LTV:CAC ratio is about 27.3 times

199 Pitch runs a social media site where users, who pay a small monthly subscription, can post business ideas. Users can 'like' each-other's ideas. These ideas can be viewed by 'business angels' – private equity investors – who decide whether or not to make an investment in the user's business. Pitch earns a commission from each 'deal' brokered by the site.

Analyse the above information and select which of the following metrics could be used by Pitch to monitor 'engagement'. Select ALL that apply.

A Average number of business ideas per user

B The number of business angels visiting

C The percentage of business angels who make a second (or subsequent) deal

D The average number of likes posted per user

E The average number of business angels expressing an interest in each idea

OBJECTIVE TEST QUESTIONS : SECTION 1

200 Glue Inc is an online credit card provider, operating under the tagline "stick with us". Unfortunately, while Glue's customers are very loyal, its staff are not. In the past five years, Glue has lost (and had to replace) nearly twenty per-cent of its employees. Apparently, the young 'millennials' employed by Glue are not finding employment with the company as engaging as the senior management team hoped.

Most of the senior staff at Glue are aged over 40, and the HR Director is 46. He has asked for your help, to address the critical issue of staff turnover.

According to the World Economic Forum, which of the following should enable Glue to become an 'employer of choice' for millennials? Select ALL that apply.

- A Work with staff to create company values
- B Increase salaries
- C Empower the workforce
- D Formulate a long-term working strategy
- E Create policies that provide a 'safe space' to work alone

201 Hirola is a 'disruptor' in the leisure travel sector. It is, in effect, an online 'travel agent'.

However, Hirola works in a completely different way from its rivals. Hirola uses Big Data analytics to examine the historic social media posts and other data of its users, who pay a very small annual subscription to Hirola. On the basis of this analysis, the Hirola app presents users with completely unique travel packages, based on their previous holidays and reviews of them. Hirola does not have any 'travel products' of its own, but combines those already offered by airlines, hotels, car hire companies and other travel firms.

The Hirola app simply asks a user for their chosen holiday dates, then delivers a 'top 5' available packages, each precisely tailored to the user's preferences. If the user selects and purchases one of the holiday packages offered, Hirola takes the user's payment and buys all of the components of the holiday package from the providers. Hirola takes a very small commission from each service provider but, as Hirola has very few staff and extremely low operating costs, it is very profitable in this highly-competitive industry.

The consultancy group Accenture wrote a report, in 2015, called "Accenture Technology Vision". This report highlighted 5 emerging trends, which were shaping the digital landscape for organisations, on which business leaders should focus when developing digital strategies.

Analyse the above description, and identify which ONE of the trends Hirola seems to be exploiting.

- A The learning organisation
- B The intelligent enterprise
- C The thinking company
- D The Platform (r)evolution

Section 2

ANSWERS TO OBJECTIVE TEST QUESTIONS

THE STRATEGY PROCESS – 15%

THE PROCESS OF STRATEGY FORMULATION

1   D

Corporate, or strategic, level strategy relates to the markets and industries that the organisation chooses to operate in, as well as other decisions that affect the organisation as a whole.

2   C

A and B are examples of corporate level strategies. D is a business strategy as it considers how to compete within a particular market. C is a practical application of the higher-level strategies, indicating that it is operational.

3   GAP 1 – C (CORPORATE), GAP 2 – B (FUNCTIONAL), GAP 3 – A (BUSINESS)

Corporate strategy examines the markets that the group operates within, which would include acquisitions and disposals. Functional strategies are practical, covering issues such as implementation. Business strategies tend to relate to specific strategic business units (SBUs), so the strategy within E would likely fall into this category.

4   A

The payroll system is simple automation of a basic business function, in order to improve efficiency. As such, it would be most likely to be seen as part of the organisation's functional strategy.

5   A

By definition.

SUBJECT E3 : STRATEGIC MANAGEMENT

6 C

C has little experience of the market, meaning that she has no ability to build on past successes – making incrementalism less useful. Her lack of experience would also suggest that freewheeling would be a risky approach. The stable nature of the market may also preclude the need for an emergent approach.

Ultimately the rational model would work well here. It will help C understand the market and guide her in the stages she needs to go through to create a strategy. It may take time, but given the unchanging nature of the market, this is time that C has to spend.

7 A, E

B refers to the emergent model, while D is logical incrementalism. C is a feature of the rational model, which gives managers a series of defined stages to follow and is therefore good for inexperienced managers.

8 GAP 1 – C (AN INCREMENTAL), GAP 2 – B (A RATIONAL)

Previously, X's strategy was simply an extension of its past activities. Going forward, it will have to plan carefully and formally for shareholder value, indicating a rational approach is needed. There is no evidence of unexpected events emerging, suggesting that the emergent approach is not needed.

9 GAP 1 – A (EFFECTIVENESS), GAP 2 – D (EFFICIENCY)

Effectiveness looks at results/outputs. The reduction in visitor numbers indicates poor effectiveness in YU. Inputs were constant (the same amount was spent on advertising as in previous years), suggesting YU was economical, but the medium used was less efficient than in previous years.

10 A, C

The traditional approach involves identifying major stakeholders and developing strategies to satisfy them. B relates to the resource-led approach, while D relates to the market-led approach.

11 B, C, E

The other duties are: to promote the success of the company, to exercise reasonable care, skill and diligence, to avoid conflicts of interests and duties.

12 B

While the diverse group of directors may possibly improve the chances of the business being run ethically (by providing a range of ethical views and opinions), the primary reason is to provide a wealth of differing experiences, ideas and viewpoints which will significantly improve the company's ability to generate and choose the best possible strategies.

13 C

Both statements are correct.

ANSWERS TO OBJECTIVE TEST QUESTIONS : SECTION 2

MISSION, VISION, VALUES AND STAKEHOLDERS

14 D

The statement is not an objective as it does not follow the SMART criteria and is too general. Non-market strategy refers to the firm's interactions with governments, regulators, NGOs and society at large, rather than its shareholders.

This leaves us with mission and vision statements. A vision is an aspiration for the future – a statement of the ideal position that the company wants to reach (i.e. 'to be the company that offers the highest value to shareholders in our industry'). The statement given is a mission – the current fundamental objective of the organisation.

15 B, D

A is the definition of a vision statement. C is incorrect – the organisation needs to publish its mission statement widely amongst stakeholders to get any real value from it.

16 C

A mission should cover why the company exists and who it exists for. It should not have specific targets or deadlines (this would turn it into an objective – like option A) and should not be too generic (unlike B). It should also consider the needs of key customers.

17 A

A vision statement is about communication with the employees (and other key stakeholders) of the organisation, which lets them see where the organisation is going in the future.

18 A, B, D

Mission statements can be an effective communication tool. If managers ignore them, or stakeholders see them as something to hide behind, then their usefulness is lost.

19 C

SMART stands for specific, measurable, attainable, relevant and timed.

20 D

The target being set is perfection. This is unlikely to be attainable in practice. The objective has no time attached to its accomplishment and it is unclear exactly how HUH plans to measure 'perfect quality' – this is too vague to be truly measurable.

However, HUH's attempt at focusing on quality is relevant – it matches what appears to be a key issue in the company's market.

21 B, D

Objectives need to be specific, measurable, attainable, relevant and time-bound. Statements that are unrealistic (such as 100% attendance), generic (such as 'the best') or not tied in to the mission (car parking) are not appropriate.

SUBJECT E3 : STRATEGIC MANAGEMENT

22   A, C, E

'Civil society' excludes governments and governmental organisations (states and organisations of states), as well as businesses (corporations and organisations formed by firms).

23   C

Groups with low interest and high power need to be kept satisfied – in other words the organisation should work to prevent them from taking an active interest in the organisation's operations.

24   A, C, D

Stakeholders identified in options A, C and D all have high interest and low power – this is the combination that suggests a 'keep informed' strategy should be adopted according to Mendelow's matrix.

LPP has little direct power, but will have a high degree of interest in K's plans for a vehicle that uses large amounts of petrol. They may undertake protests against K to try and affect other stakeholders, such as governments and the media/general public.

K's sales staff will be highly interested in the proposed job losses as many of them will be directly affect by the strategy. However, given the lack of unionisation and low skill levels, they are likely to have little power to influence K's strategy.

The same can be said of F Ltd. K's two-seater cars are extremely important to their business, but they make up a tiny percentage of K's sales – giving them very limited power to affect K's operations.

The government of country H, on the other hand, seems to have high power over the operation of K's key factories. Their level of interest is perhaps arguable – they are taking an active interest in monitoring the compliance of factories based in country H, but are unlikely to take action unless the rules are not being complied with. They could therefore be classified as either key players or 'keep satisfied' stakeholders.

25   A

Employees will be interested as the move affects their livelihoods, but have little power to stop the move. Customers will have little interest as it will not affect their interaction with the company. The UK government is likely to have little interest or power in the move of the company as it is not breaking any laws. Major shareholders may be very interested as it impacts upon their investment. However, they would be key players.

26   D

The CGFSA is likely to be classed as high power. It is backed by central government and can levy fines and penalties for non-compliance.

As long as Pirlo met all appropriate legislation, it would have low interest in the company, suggesting that it would need to be kept satisfied (per Mendelow's matrix). However, Pirlo's admission that it has broken food safety laws will mean that the CGFSA would take an active interest in the company, moving to become a key player.

ANSWERS TO OBJECTIVE TEST QUESTIONS : **SECTION 2**

27 A

OOB controls a key resource that RRL needs – its drivers.

28 A

Side payments occur when some form of compensation is offered in order to help resolve conflict.

29 B

Non-market strategy looks at key stakeholders outside of the organisation's traditional markets. This may include regulators, NGOs, the media and society at large.

GOVERNANCE, ETHICS AND CORPORATE SOCIAL RESPONSIBILITY

30 C, D, E

A strong CSR approach may, in fact, increase costs as the organisation has to source its goods more carefully. There is no reason why a strong CSR approach would speed up decision making in the organisation – in fact it is likely to use up management time that could be spent helping to earn the business higher profits. However, CSR often helps to attract both customers and staff, and reduces that chance that governments will be forced to regulate against unethical business behaviour in future.

31 C

V is only concerned with the returns of the organisation for himself and his business partners. He seems to be taking a short-term view, with regard only for reducing costs. He has made no effort to provide more than the legal minimum provisions for his staff. This would indicate he is at the lowest level of Johnson, Scholes and Whittington's ethical stances – short term shareholder interest. Note that there is evidence that this approach is doing long-term damage to the business.

32 D

The key here is to note that the organisation sees financial concerns as secondary to its mission and objectives, which appear to be focused on minimising the company's environmental impact.

33 A, C

The definition in B is that of CSR – not sustainability. Sustainability and CSR may cost more in the short term, but it is possible to make short-term savings. For example, becoming more energy efficient could allow an organisation to save money on fuel bills in the short term.

34 A

H is responding to demands from external groups relating to corporate social responsibility. However, he is yet to seek out ways of going beyond these requirements, indicating that he has yet to reach the proaction philosophy.

SUBJECT E3 : STRATEGIC MANAGEMENT

35   C, D, E

The other part of corporate social responsibility is philanthropic responsibilities.

36   **NOTE: ELEMENTS CAN BE PLACED IN ANY ORDER UNDER EACH HEADING**

Strategy and oversight	Execution and alignment	Performance and reporting
Board and senior management commitment	Extensive and effective sustainability training	Champions to promote sustainability and celebrate success
	Ensuring sustainability is the responsibility of everyone within the organisation	Including sustainability targets and objectives in performance appraisal

37   B

Integrity implies fair dealing and truthfulness. For J to be associated with inaccurate or misleading statements would breach his integrity.

38   A

Objectivity means ensuring that business/professional judgement is not compromised by bias or conflict of interest.

39   C

Information obtained in a business relationship must not be disclosed outside the organisation unless there is a professional right or duty to disclose it. It must not be used for personal advantage.

40   B, D, C, A, E

Remember, if an ethical dilemma occurs, a professional accountant must first ensure they fully understand the situation. They should then follow the relevant internal procedures to deal with the problem within their organisation. If this fails, they can contact their professional body for help. If a solution cannot be found, they may have to withdraw from the engagement to ensure they preserve their ethics.

41   B, C, E

These are the three major reasons for disclosure of confidential information to third parties.

ANSWERS TO OBJECTIVE TEST QUESTIONS : SECTION 2

ANALYSING THE ORGANISATIONAL ECOSYSTEM – 20%

EXTERNAL ENVIRONMENTAL ANALYSIS

42 A, C, D, E

Environmental analysis is unlikely to help L identify its resources as this would require internal strategic analysis, rather than external.

43 GAP 1 – F (ENVIRONMENTAL), GAP 2 – C (LEGAL), GAP 3 – E (TECHNOLOGICAL), GAP 4 – A (POLITICAL)

Make sure you are comfortable classifying issues within a PESTEL analysis, as it is a key external analysis model.

44 A, B

PESTEL looks at the macro-environment of the organisation. While this can include certain aspects of the organisation's industry, this is not its focus. It also does not examine internal issues.

45 D

A is likely to be technological, while B and C are social. Note that D could also be classified as a legal issue within PESTEL analysis – however this is not a separate category within PESTEL and would be included in 'political'.

46 A, B, D

Each of these sources of information is likely to help the company to shed some light on its potential operations in country X.

47 A, C, D

B is part of Porter's Diamond model, while E is likely to be part of PESTEL analysis. The missing forces are power of suppliers and rivalry amongst competitors.

48 GAP 1 – B (THREAT OF NEW ENTRANTS), GAP 2 – D (POWER OF SUPPLIERS)

The new bureaucratic process is making it more complicated for organisations to start up in X's market, increasing barriers to entry and thereby reducing the threat of new entrants. X has managed to tie in its staff – who are key suppliers to the organisation. This reduces their power to leave and move to one of X's rivals.

49 C

The competitive rivalry will be high in Q's industry as all rivals are similar sizes and manufacture similar products, making it difficult for any one manufacturer to dominate the market or gain market share. The large number of patents will make it hard for new entrants to break into the market, while the fact that Q buys from a large number of small suppliers suggests that supplier power is also low. Finally, there is no information relating to substitutes in the scenario.

SUBJECT E3 : STRATEGIC MANAGEMENT

50 C

A would indicate low buyer power – customers have to purchase Y's products if they want the special features they offer. B also suggests low power – if Y has few rivals it means customers have less choice. C indicates that customers have knowledge of Y's rivals prices and product features. This increases the likelihood that they will switch supplier, increasing their power. Finally, the requirement to have car insurance is unlikely to force customers to use Y (though clearly it increases the size of Y's potential market).

51

	Increased	Decreased
Power of customers	1	2
Threat of substitutes		
Threat of new entrants		2, 3

The threat of backwards integration by a customer (i.e. the possibility they may purchase Z) gives them more power over the company and the decisions it will make. Z and its rivals have managed to lock in all major distribution channels – this will make it harder for new entrants to sell their products, as will Z's ability to keep costs (and therefore prices) low due to its significant economies of scale.

52 B, C

The fact that OFG has few rivals does not prevent the Five Forces model from being of use. In addition, OFG appears to be a profit-seeking organisation. This means that the Five Forces model's focus on industry profitability is entirely appropriate for the business.

Note that Porter's Five Forces may also be inappropriate for OFG as it ignore the influence of government (very important for OFG) and is of limited usefulness for competence-based businesses such as OFG (where the value is added through internal competences such as R&D/innovation).

53 A, B, D

'Up front capital costs' are a barrier to entry, as is 'differentiation'. Rivals will lose market share as a result of X's new core competence. Customers will experience a 'switching cost' (poorer service levels) should they move from X to a rival.

54 A, E

The changes will have no significant effect on substitution or the Bargaining Power of Pink's suppliers. Rivalry is not affected as, at present, none of the firms in Pink's industry use bots.

The Threat of New Entrants will have risen as firms not currently operating in Pink's sector, but which use bots in the relevant functions, can enter without an investment in this area.

The Bargaining Power of those customers using bots for procurement and inbound logistics will have risen, as they gain access to better information and cheaper processes.

ANSWERS TO OBJECTIVE TEST QUESTIONS : **SECTION 2**

55 A

The product is still experiencing strong growth. This has been reduced, however, by large numbers of new competitors entering the market. This would indicate that the TT155 is still in the growth stage. It has yet to reach maturity as it is still growing strongly. It is certainly not in decline.

56 A

These are typical strategies for an organisation moving into decline – the goal is to get as much return from the product as possible while it is still viable.

57 B

Maturity involves a stable market with relatively high numbers of competitors. Price matching (or going-rate pricing) would be most suitable here.

58 D

Form competitors sell products that satisfy the same needs as ours (and target the same market segments) but which have significantly different technical specifications – such as tents and caravans.

59 A3, B1, C2, D4

By definition.

60 C

Stochastic rivals have no predictable pattern to their responses – like GG. Laid back indicates no response, selective competitors only respond to attacks on certain markets, while tigers always respond aggressively.

61 A

The graduates are an important factor that are needed by X. Be careful – the question specified the graduates themselves. The university would be classified as a related and supporting industry.

62 D

V's intense domestic rivalry is likely to help it be competitive in its future expansion.

63 B, D, E

B, D and E are all other businesses that SP Ltd is likely to need in order to operate successfully in country G. A is linked to demand conditions, while C is a factor condition.

SUBJECT E3 : STRATEGIC MANAGEMENT

64 A2, B3, C1, D4

Poor eyesight in country F indicates potentially high demand for HGY's services. HGY's monopoly in its current home country could mean that it lacks the ability to break into a (possibly) more competitive market like country F as it is inexperienced in adopting strategies needed to deal with these competitors. Empty premises are a factor that HGY needs to open its chain of opticians. Equipment suppliers would be a related/supporting industry that is lacking country F.

65 A

The Internet of Me – users are being placed at the centre of digital experiences through apps and services being personalised.

STRATEGIC NETWORKS AND PLATFORMS

66 A

AAA has two major suppliers in the scenario. Firstly – its engines are all sourced from a single car manufacturer, which is likely to give the supplier a high level of power as AAA is reliant on them for a key component. AAA's other supplier – BBB – is also likely to have high power due to the highly specialised and essential nature of the work they undertake.

67 B, C, E

Downstream supply chains refer to anything between an organisation and the end-consumer of its products or services. For a baker, this would involve the retailers that sell its products, as well the final consumer. The farmers and wheat wholesalers that H obtains its raw materials from would be part of H's upstream supply chain.

68 A

QII's customers need to have sufficient cash to purchase QII's circuit boards, while QII's suppliers – both the mines and the processing companies – have to make sufficient profit to make it worth them continuing to supplying palladium. If QII drives the price down too far, they may find that mines and processing companies go out of business, leading to a scarcity of Palladium on the open market.

69 B, C

The new system will not increase KKB's competitive advantage as it currently has no competition in its market due to its exclusive franchise. It will also not reduce KKB's exposure to technology risks as it is moving from a manual to a more automated system. However, e-procurement will help KKB to scan the market and find other suppliers of diesel, reducing its over-reliance on its single current supplier. This may also enable it to reduce its inventory of diesel as it is more likely to be able to find a supplier quickly if its levels are running low.

ANSWERS TO OBJECTIVE TEST QUESTIONS : **SECTION 2**

70

Transaction marketing	Relationship marketing
Concentrates on products	Service quality is a critical success factor
Motorbike and scooter quality is a critical success factor	Requires detailed knowledge of customer needs
Little emphasis on repeat rental	

Note: answers can be in any order as long as they are under the correct heading.

71 A, C, E

The other three are: referral markets, supplier markets and recruitment markets.

72 B

The new application is influencing viewers on what to watch – and if it suggests that a VVC programme is good to watch, it is likely to boost VVC's viewing figures and therefore its advertising revenue. The application is not an actual customer of VVC's so A is incorrect. The application does not appear to be written by VVC, so it is not internal and, finally, it does not link to VVC's ability to recruit staff.

73 D

Just because a customer is earning a significant amount of revenue does not mean that it is profitable or that it should be retained by the company. As can be seen from the statistics, while Customer 3 is the largest by revenue, it takes far more sales visits and rush orders than the other customers. As these costs cannot be passed on to its customers, Customer 3 may be the least profitable of the three and ABC may consider eliminating it. B and C are unlikely to be correct – it appears that ABC may become uncompetitive if it raises its prices or simply ceases to offer rush deliveries.

74 D

HGH is creating a new stage in the supply chain – sitting between the takeaway and the consumer. Disintermediation involves removing a stage in the supply chain (such as selling direct to the end consumer) and countermediation would occur if one of HGH's rivals set up their own, similar intermediary to compete with HGH.

75 B, D

Downstream management refers to anything that is done by JAF to manage relationships with customers and/or consumers. Option C refers to upstream supply management (with JAF's suppliers). Option A is not suitable for JAF. As JAF sells to individual consumers on the high street, there is no opportunity for it to design an EDI system to link its computer systems with those of its customers.

SUBJECT E3 : STRATEGIC MANAGEMENT

76 B

Ego, or status, needs are those that allow the user to 'show off' or highlight their status to others. Attending a bar which has the reputation for being extremely expensive is likely to fulfil this within its users.

77 A

By definition. Reciprocal buying is where organisations buy goods from each other, propensity modelling refers to evaluating customer behaviour and then making recommendations for their future purchases and transaction marketing is where an organisation focuses on the product it sells rather than building a relationship with its customers.

RESOURCES AND VALUE CREATION WITHIN THE ORGANISATIONAL ECOSYSTEM

78 C

The system provides management with important information to help them with their strategic decision making. It does not relate to the management themselves, or the markets the business operates in (though it helps the business access these markets successfully). The system would also not be included within make-up, which refers to the organisation's brand.

79 A, C

Threshold competences are the things an organisation needs to do just to be able to compete in a given market. They do not convey competitive advantage, meaning that B is incorrect. D is also incorrect as this statement is the wrong way round – core competences tend to become threshold over time as customer tastes change and rivals copy them. Finally E is also incorrect – core competences are what the organisation does well, while critical success factors are what the organisation needs to do well to be successful. Ideally they should match, but they may not.

80

	CSF		Related KPI
1	High levels of customer satisfaction	6	No more than 2% of customers submit complaints
5	Affordable rental charges	4	Prices must be within 5% of the average charge by rivals
7	Well-maintained vehicles	3	Vehicle breakdowns occur less than 1 per 100 rental days
8	Excellent customer service	2	Answer telephone calls within 5 rings

Note: CSFs can be in any order – as long as they are linked to the related KPI.

ANSWERS TO OBJECTIVE TEST QUESTIONS : SECTION 2

81

	CSF		Related KPI
1	Reasonable prices	8	Average contract charges to be lower than that of two largest rivals
3	Customer loyalty	7	90% customer retention at the end of their contract
5	Happy customers	2	An average score of 4.5 out of 5 (or higher) on customer satisfaction surveys
6	Good quality network provision	4	Less than 1 in 50 calls should fail due to network problems

Note: CSFs can be in any order – as long as they are linked to the related KPI.

82 A

B will not help improve quality itself and therefore does not link to the CSF identified. C is not specific – how will the company decide if 'quality' is improved by 15%? D has no measurable target for the amount of training that will be undertaken.

83 A, B, C

The other source, according to Rockart, was 'temporal organisational factors'.

84 C

Temporal factors are those areas that are unusually causing concern because they are unacceptable and need attention. While the fine is triggered by the government (which is part of the wider environment), the fact that the problem is unusual and short-term indicates it is a temporal issue.

85 C

By definition.

86 A, B, E

The other secondary activity is human resource management. The remaining options are primary activities.

87 C

Inbound logistics refers to the receipt, handling and storage of inputs. The Managing Director (MD) is referring to procurement – the sourcing of inputs. The MD seems to understand operations – they would indeed be the printing functions within QOI – however he doesn't seem to understand outbound logistics. This refers to the storage and distribution of the organisation's final product – the MD discusses promotion, which would be part of sales.

SUBJECT E3 : STRATEGIC MANAGEMENT

88   A4, B3, C1, D2

For a toy manufacturer like F, dealing with customer complaints is a post-sale activity, which will therefore be classified as service. Budgeting is a central planning function and is therefore likely to be part of the firm's infrastructure. Staff training is the responsibility of the human resource management function, while automated inventory control for raw materials will be inbound logistics.

89   B

The system helps manage the finished loaves, indicating that it refers to outbound logistics. It does not manage the raw materials (or ingredients), indicating that it will not help inbound logistics. It also is used after JJE bakes the loaves of bread, so it cannot be part of operations.

90   A3, B4, C2, D1

Don't forget that the value chain can apply to service industries as well as manufacturers. In this case, the value chain tracks the movement of information through the firm – inputs from clients, followed by the use of this during trials.

91   B

For YF, inbound logistics involves gathering and storing information about the patient. This is done through the central database. Operations then involves deciding on a diagnosis for the patient – which the new system will help the qualified operators to do. Outbound logistics is then passing this information on clearly to the customer and ensuring they know what to do next (in this case that is accomplished for the majority of patients by way of an email).

92   A, B, D

A is correct as the value shop has the same secondary activities as the more common value chain model. B and D are also stages of the value shop, along with problem solving and problem finding and acquisition. C is a primary activity of the value chain. E is not part of the value shop or value chain.

93   D

Human resource management looks at ensuring the right employees are selected and managed throughout the company's operations.

94   B

The new entrants are an external issue and they are potentially going to damage QOS's market share. They would therefore be classified as a threat.

95   D, E

A is either an opportunity or a threat, while B and C are simply facts – there is no evidence that they are good or bad. D and E both refer to internal issues that will benefit the organisation – strong systems and management awareness of business needs can both be classified as strengths.

ANSWERS TO OBJECTIVE TEST QUESTIONS : SECTION 2

96 B

The first bullet point is incorrect. While corporate appraisal (SWOT) will include industry-wide issues facing the company, it is not the main (or sole) focus of the model. Industry analysis is typically undertaken using Porter's Five Forces. The other two statements are correct.

97 D

The growing market for office chairs represents a growth opportunity for PAG. PAG is already skilled in chair manufacture, and has an excellent reputation, suggesting that chair manufacture is a strength of its business. This would therefore bode well for their expansion into this new market segment.

98 A

This is an area where the company is under attack, but is currently also a weak area. Such an issue could cause major problems for the organisation and would therefore usually be prioritised. A defensive strategy would be crucial for the organisation to develop.

GENERATING STRATEGIC OPTIONS – 15%

FRAMEWORK FOR GENERATING STRATEGIC OPTIONS

99 B

Gap 1 is referred to as the diversification gap, while gap 3 is the efficiency gap.

100 A, D

The expansion gap can be closed by adopting an effectiveness drive – this involves market penetration strategies (like A), market or product development strategies (like D) or diversification. B and C are both parts of an efficiency drive (an attempt to reduce costs), which would be part of closing an efficiency gap.

101 C

Don't get confused between the Delphi model and a think tank. In the Delphi model, experts never meet.

102 A, B, C

The other two parts of the 5Cs are – co-ordination and consensus.

103 B

The scenario is describing exactly what derived demand is designed to help accomplish. It is used to analyse a particular aspect of economic activity (i.e. the demand for electronics components) and use this to derive the demand for something else (i.e. demand for WEJ's metals).

SUBJECT E3 : STRATEGIC MANAGEMENT

104 C, E, B, D, F, A, G

By definition.

105 A, C

Scenario planning is all about identifying key high-impact, high-uncertainty factors in the organisation's environment. A falls into this category – it is uncertain whether the government will put in place minimum wage legislation and this could have a significant impact on the company's profits. IOS definitely needs a contingency plan for this, so it would likely be built into the scenario planning process.

B is relatively low impact (thanks to IOS's insurance) and low uncertainty (IOS seems confident that it will have to pay the fine), so no further analysis is needed.

C is another factor that is high impact (the cost of gold rising sharply could cause a fall in profits) and high uncertainty (the movement in gold prices is uncertain, as is the likelihood of a recession). Again, IOS may wish to consider contingency plans here – such as hedging against gold price movements.

Finally D appears to be highly uncertain (it is not clear how long the CEO will stay with the company), but low impact (the remaining Board of Directors is capable of minimising disruption to the company), so again this is unlikely to be a necessary factor that needs building into scenario planning for IOS.

106 A, B, D

Note that C and E are incorrect – scenario planning arguably helps the organisation to reduce its risk profile by planning for potential future problems, while the act of building scenarios and creating contingency plans actively encourages managers to think creatively.

107 A

The statements relating to game theory are all correct.

108 C

The house-building project, while unprofitable, will enable VAGH to access more profitable opportunities in the future. This is an example of an option to follow on.

109 A, B, D

C is incorrect – the definition given is that of an option to follow on, not to delay.

ANSWERS TO OBJECTIVE TEST QUESTIONS : **SECTION 2**

STRATEGIC OPTIONS

110   GAP 1 – C (FOCUS), GAP 2 – A (DIFFERENTIATION)

The lack of market segmentation information means that JAV will be unable to reliably target any particular segment (or niche) within the wider market. The information about competitor activities also indicates that the market is uninterested in low-cost items, so a cost leadership approach is unlikely to be successful for JAV. It needs to adopt a differentiation approach and find some way of enabling its laptops to stand out from its rivals.

111   A, C, D

Cost leadership will not necessarily allow TIDL to improve its reputation (in fact it may cause it to fall given the possible reduction in quality that TIDL must offer). E refers to a focus strategy rather than a cost leadership approach. Lower costs will allow a higher margin than rivals and allow TIDL to cut prices in the event of a price war, as well as offering its goods at a lower, penetration price than its rivals.

112   D

Spiral has differentiated itself within the small niche market for walking equipment in the area. Adopting a focus approach can enable an organisation to charge a premium for its products as they are tailored to the specific needs of its market.

113   C

SOC has little that gives it a competitive advantage. While its costs are low, they are no lower than those of its rivals – which explains the similar pricing structures. It also offers similar unbranded goods to its rivals, suggesting that it is not differentiated. SOC is also not gaining competitive advantage merely from selling to a small sub-set of the market. According to Porter, it would therefore be classed as stuck in the middle.

114   A, B, E

The smartphones market for the over 60s is unproven. Uptake has been slow to date – it may simply be that this demographic has little interest in purchasing smartphones, meaning that A is correct. B is also correct – CHO has little experience of designing a product for this niche market. It therefore needs to undertake significant research into their needs before developing its new phone.

C is incorrect – given the relatively low incomes received by many in the target market, it seems unlikely that CHO will be able to sell its products at a premium – even if they are tailored to the precise needs of the over 60s. D is an advantage of CHO's strategy – not a risk.

Finally, E is correct – if inflation rates rise, this will reduce the amount of disposable income of CHO's target niche. This is likely to mean that they will be unable to afford to purchase the smartphone, making CHO's product unattractive.

115   C

Market development refers to a strategy of selling existing products to new markets.

SUBJECT E3 : STRATEGIC MANAGEMENT

116 D

The product that HUT is selling is fundamentally the same as it always was – HUT is simply trying to increase demand and sell more units to its existing markets.

117 A4, B1, C3, D2

MAH already sells food products – selling some of these through new outlets (i.e. to travellers on the motorways) is an example of market development – existing products to new markets.

MAH's clothing advertising campaign is trying to sell more of its existing clothing lines to its current markets. This would be a classic example of market development.

Selling electricals is new for MAH – but it's selling them in its existing stores. This would indicate product development – new products for existing customers.

Finally, MAH is planning on offering limited online banking services. Banking is a new area for MAH and it will be offering these online, likely targeting new market segments. This would most likely be classified as diversification.

118 B

Backwards vertical integration refers to the acquisition of an organisation's suppliers (as is the case for VAT). Forward vertical integration would involve the purchase of an organisation's customers.

119 A, C

Diversification is often the only way an organisation can grow if its current markets are saturated – especially if it has excess cash and resources. Diversification will also reduce the organisation's risk by removing the dependency on the organisation's current markets. However it is unlikely to free up management time (quite the contrary – expanding into a new market is likely to be extremely time consuming), and is unlikely to increase the organisation's synergies as it is into an unrelated industry.

120 A, C, E

The acquisition of BLP will help to ensure that NET continues to have a ready supply of iron ore – especially important as other mines are being bought up by NET's rivals. This prevents NET from being locked out of the market (i.e. unable to source raw materials as they are all controlled by NET's rivals). NET's acquisition will also enable it to enjoy economies of avoiding the market – costs such as negotiation and finding suppliers will be reduced.

However, NET is tying itself to BLP as a sole supplier. As NET is used to shopping around for the cheapest source of ore, the purchase of BLP is likely to limit its ability to do this. In addition, the acquisition is unlikely to allow BLP to differentiate itself in the market, as many of BLP's rivals are already doing the same.

121 D

Horizontal diversification includes expansion into competing or complementary products. In this case, the company sees the new production lines as helping UY offer a full product range to the market.

ANSWERS TO OBJECTIVE TEST QUESTIONS : SECTION 2

MAKING STRATEGIC CHOICES – 15%

PORTFOLIO ANALYSIS

122 A

A star product has high growth and high market share, placing JoyB in quadrant 1.

123 B, C

Holding strategies involve the organisation working to maintain the product's current position in its market. This is only sensible if the product already has a good market share – i.e. if it is a star or a cash cow.

124 A3, B4, C1, D2

Alpha is the market leader in a fast growing industry, making it a star product. Bravo's market is also fast growing, but it has a relatively low market share, suggesting it is a question mark. Charlie has a small share of a slow growth market, suggesting a dog which should be divested. Delta has a very large share of a declining market, suggesting a cash cow.

125 C

Given the fact that Darz is no longer fashionable and has been largely replaced by more modern gel detergents, it is unlikely that SOH will be able to easily hold its current market share without significant investment. This does not seem sensible in a mature market.

As mentioned above, a building strategy – where SOH tries to aggressively grow market share through investment in the product also seems a poor strategic decision. The market is saturated and it seems unlikely that Darz will become a market leader.

However, divesting the product also seems inappropriate. While sales are low, the product is still generating profits for now and helps to support other sales through its use of the SOH brand name.

Therefore SOH should look at ways of harvesting – reducing costs as far as possible to maximise the profitability of Darz for as long as possible.

126 C

A is incorrect – ARC is a star, BUY is a question mark and GUD is a dog product on the BCG matrix. This indicates at least some progression within TIH's portfolio – GUD appears to be a product towards the end of its life, ARC is probably in the growth stage of its life cycle and BUY is in the introduction stage. This would suggest that they are unlikely to all decline at the same time.

However, TIH seems to lack a cash cow. Given the funds required to develop, launch and grow BUY and the costs of defending ARC's market position, it is likely that TIH is facing liquidity problems.

While BUY has a low market share, it is in a high growth industry. Given TIH's limited product range, it probably needs to invest in this product (if it has the funds to do so). Note that a low market share is not necessarily a reason in itself to divest a product.

SUBJECT E3 : STRATEGIC MANAGEMENT

STRATEGY EVALUATION

127 B, C, E

If GHA has limited access to funds, it will likely find it difficult to afford the purchase price of one of its rivals. Organic growth can be undertaken more slowly, as and when the business can afford it. Organic growth will also avoid GHA having problems with government legislation – as there are only three companies providing surveyor training in the country, the government may step in to avoid GHA becoming too dominant in the market. Finally, if GHA has a very different corporate culture to its rivals, it will make acquisition and integration of their businesses very difficult.

The other two options would encourage GHA to adopt an acquisitions approach. If GHA is under pressure for fast increases in sales, acquisition may be the best approach. GHA may also want to acquire a rival as a defensive strategy to prevent an even more dangerous competitor entering the market.

128 B

Given the size of the investment involved, it seems sensible to have a formal agreement between the two companies. Only a joint venture would seem to meet the needs of both parties and enable them to collaborate on the design and launch of the new facilities.

129 C

QQH is the classic scenario for a franchise – allowing rapid expansion, but ensuring tight control of that expansion, with minimal outlay for the franchisor. However, it may be too early for QQH to consider franchising. QQH only has two restaurants and they are both in the capital city. It is unlikely to have a well-known brand and this would be vital to attracting franchisees willing to pay for the right to trade as QQH. In addition, QQH's management is inexperienced and would be unlikely to be able to ensure control of a rapidly expanding chain of franchised restaurants, all of whom will be expecting some form of central support. Ultimately, QQH should consider growing organically for the near future until it has built a more developed brand and a stronger management structure.

130 A

Multinational organisations are organisations that co-ordinate their activities across national boundaries in order to maximise efficiency. Note that the company still has a defined 'home' country, suggesting that it is not a transnational organisation.

131 GAP 1 – B (IS NOT), GAP 2 – B (IS NOT), GAP 3 – A (IS)

Suitability examines whether a given strategy matches the circumstances of the organisation. While the CEO's proposal would potentially allow the charity to return to earning surpluses, it fundamentally misses the purpose of the organisation. By eliminating the roles of its existing staff, BOQ will not be 'supporting citizens of country F who are in need'.

The proposal is certainly not acceptable – BOQ's staff are unlikely to agree with it and, in all likelihood, neither are BOQ's other trustees.

The proposal is, however, feasible. There are no legal issues and BOQ's CEO noted that there would be no union entanglements.

ANSWERS TO OBJECTIVE TEST QUESTIONS : SECTION 2

132 D

The CEO's proposal is unlikely to be suitable. Not only does the suggestion not play to the organisation's current strengths (i.e. the excellent quality service and focus on business class), but the budget market is already crowded, meaning that CHA is unlikely to be able to compete here. This would not help it increase its revenue or profitability.

The proposal is clearly unacceptable to the stakeholders in the scenario. The Board of Directors and the unionised staff are all highly resistant to the plans. It is also unlikely to be acceptable to CHA's core customers – business class customers who expect a high level of service and comfort.

Finally the proposal seems to lack feasibility. The company only has a small cash surplus, while the re-launch of the company is likely to need significant expenditure (i.e. advertising, staff redundancy costs). In addition, the strong reaction against the plans by powerful stakeholders (unionised staff and directors) will make it extremely difficult for the CEO to implement.

Note that B cannot be a correct answer – for the strategy to be accepted it must be suitable, feasible AND acceptable. If any one of the three is not present, the strategy would be rejected.

133 D

Acceptability is all about ensuring that a strategy is acceptable to key stakeholders. The best way of analysing this would be by using Mendelow's power interest matrix to identify which stakeholders would be affected by/need to be taken into account when examining the strategy.

STRATEGIC CONTROL – 20%

PERFORMANCE MANAGEMENT SYSTEMS

134 A, C

The new measures seem to downgrade the need for staff to provide a helpful service for callers and stress the importance of speed – speed in answering and rapidly dealing with caller queries. This could confuse call centre staff as the new measures for speed may conflict with the third measure – number of complaints. Staff may be tempted to deal abruptly or unhelpfully with callers simply to reduce call times, which will enable them to achieve 2 out of their three bonus targets. This could lead to a rise in complaints.

Note that performance measurement mix changes may change the culture of the organisation, but this is not a reason for avoiding making these changes. The new culture may be better and help the organisation get closer to its strategic objectives.

In addition, the fact that there are no financial measures in the mix does not necessarily make it inappropriate. Q's goal as a council is likely to be about offering an effective service – finances may be secondary.

SUBJECT E3 : STRATEGIC MANAGEMENT

135 C

ROCE is calculated as profit before interest and tax divided by capital employed (shareholders' funds plus long-term debt). Reduced levels of equity would likely increase ROCE as it would reduce shareholders' funds, as would the payment of large dividends. Improved cost control would be expected to increase ROCE. Note that ROCE is a key investor ratio. The fact that it has fallen would suggest that the company is a less attractive investment now than it was a year ago, as it is returning less per pound of investor capital.

136 C, D

Including non-financial measures will make it more complex for POG to measure performance. This will likely lead to rising performance measurement costs. In addition, if POG want to reduce subjectivity in performance measurement, including non-financial measures will not help with this, as they can be very subjective (especially when looking at fashion design and retail). Given that POG operates in three very different areas – manufacturing, retail and design – it is unlikely that POG will find it easy to have consistent non-financial measures across the entire organisation.

However, POG will wish to include more non-financial measures given the increasing quality problems, and the fact that many staff members don't understand company finances may also suggest that they will find non-financial measures easier to comprehend and more motivational.

137 A3, B1, C2, D4

Targets set around profitability are most likely to be classified as financial in nature. Learning and growth includes innovation – so new packages offered to customers would be an example of this. Reduction in complaints is a classic option for the measurement of the customer perspective, while the number of dropped calls relates to the quality and efficiency of X's infrastructure, which would be included within X's internal business processes perspective.

138 A, C

A and C are both related to the internal processes of CRR – calculating and submitting client tax returns. Note that it is possible that, potentially, either of these measures could also be used as customer perspective indicators, but this is not requested by this question. Options B and D are both linked to learning and growth.

139 D

O is a charity and will therefore be uninterested in its profit margins or the return offered to its investor (via the ROCE). C relates to the 'learning and growth' perspective of the balanced scorecard. However, O will need to ensure that it is using its funds (such as its advertising and fund raising budgets) as efficiently as possible to ensure it can continue its operations.

140 A, B, E

The Balance Scorecard (BS) includes a range of measures – including longer-term non-financial measures. It also allows each part of the organisation to create its own indicators.

ANSWERS TO OBJECTIVE TEST QUESTIONS : **SECTION 2**

141 B

The remaining factors are internal efficiency measures.

142 A

This is a 'market' critical success factor, so it is therefore included within the 'business units' level of the pyramid. Business operating systems refer to the internal systems and processes within the organisation. Department and work centres refer to the day to day operational measures that can be used to monitor the status of the higher level measures.

143 B, C, E

The dimensions, in full, are: profit, competitiveness, quality, resource utilisation, flexibility and innovation. A and D refer to the other two building blocks within Fitzgerald and Moon's model.

144 GAP 1 – C (STANDARDS), GAP 2 – B (REWARDS)

Standards are the specific targets set by management in each of the dimensions (the organisation's goals). They need to be seen as achievable or they will fail to motivate staff. The rewards the business offers for completion of these standards needs to be significant enough to motivate staff, as well as only relating to things that are within the control of the staff members being assessed.

145 GAP 1 – C (COMPETITIVE), GAP 2 – B (INTERNAL), GAP 3 – A (PROCESS)

Competitive benchmarking is likely to provide innovative ideas to the organisation, but it can be difficult to convince a successful rival to share their secrets. As internal benchmarking focuses on other parts of the same organisation, this type of benchmarking often fails to provide any particularly radical new ideas. Process benchmarking can be difficult as there may be few, if any, non-competing businesses that have the same core processes as our organisation. It is therefore often undertaken for non-core activities.

146 D

Competitive benchmarking is not likely to be useful to KV as it is already the dominant market leader. Internal benchmarking would help each store to learn how to behave like the best stores within KV, ensuring that the highest levels of customer service are applied throughout the business.

147 B, C

Remember that SVA focuses on improving the seven key value drivers – sales growth, life of the project, operating margin, working capital, cost of capital, asset investment and taxation. B and C are consistent with this. A is a feature of EVA, not SVA. D is a drawback of SVA and EVA, as they do not take account of such intangible assets.

SUBJECT E3 : STRATEGIC MANAGEMENT

148 B

Your colleague's understanding of Triple Bottom Line (TBL) appears fairly good. The only mistake she has made is that measuring the various aspects of TBL (such as the company's impact on the planet and people) can be very subjective. Often the measures are difficult and time-consuming to monitor and report on.

149 A, B, D

There is no obvious reason why discussing the proposals with staff would reduce the risk of them acting unethically (e.g. forging absentee sheets) in a bid to improve their bonus.

150 B, C

Staff do not seem to think that they cannot achieve the target set. Instead they have already identified ways of achieving the target by 'hurrying through their existing jobs'. This is likely to cause a fall in the quality of the work that employees undertake, leading to sub-optimal behaviour. In addition, staff are unlikely to be concerned about whether they meet the stretch targets or not – there is no benefit to them for meeting the target, other than an ill-defined 'benefit to the whole business'. The stretch targets would help the firm to clear its backlog, so it could be seen as an appropriate area for J to set targets in.

151 A, B, C, D, E

All of these are included. The other two guiding principles are Reliability and completeness, and Consistency and comparability.

152 A

Institutional is not one of the six capitals. The other three are Financial, Human, and Social and Relationship.

ANSWERS TO OBJECTIVE TEST QUESTIONS : **SECTION 2**

CHANGE MANAGEMENT

153

	Indirect triggers		Direct triggers
A	Increased government health and safety legislation relating to tanning stores	C	TYS, a new tanning company, is offering tanning to customers at heavy discounts
B	Recession in country F, leading to a fall in consumer disposable income	D	WAM – suppliers of sun beds in country F has closed, leaving only one company offering the tanning beds that PI uses in its stores
E	Tanning has started to be seen as unfashionable by consumers in country F		

Note: answers can be in any order as long as they are under the correct heading.

Remember that indirect triggers are general environmental issues (as would be found by PEST analysis). Direct triggers are those that relate to the organisation's industry and that would be identified as part of the organisation's Five Forces analysis.

154 B

Adaptation refers to an incremental change which is a re-alignment (i.e. a slow, relatively minor change). On the diagram, this is quadrant 2.

155 C

Staff are about to see a fundamental change in the way they operate and their corporate culture. This is likely to be perceived as a transformational change. In addition, OOO wish to enact these changes quickly, suggesting a 'big bang'. This would suggest that staff will see the change as a revolution.

156 A, B

A is a common problem with change analysis – different stakeholders perceive the change differently. It may be that AVV's strategic managers see the change as a transformation as it will have a serious impact on how and where they decide to spend their resources. Fundraising staff, however, will see little change to their role and therefore may see it as a simple realignment.

B is also correct – changes in legislation would typically be identified through a PEST analysis, which identifies indirect triggers for change.

C is incorrect – the scenario makes it clear that the change is rapid at AVV, indicating that it is 'big bang' rather than incremental.

D is also incorrect – again, evolutionary change is slow, while AVV's appears to be rapid. In addition, a forced, reactive change is typically a description of revolution rather than evolution.

SUBJECT E3 : STRATEGIC MANAGEMENT

157 A, C, E

The other elements of the cultural web are: power structure, control systems, stories and myths and organisational structure. B and D are elements of McKinsey's 7S model.

158 C

'Stories and myths' refers to what employees are talking about with each other. This is a strong indication of the organisation's core beliefs might be and can be a very important part of the cultural web analysis. In this case, the employees' stories seem to underline the need for continuity of practice within Hexagon.

159

Hard		Soft	
C	Structure	A	Staff
E	Strategy	B	Skills
G	Systems	D	Shared values
		F	Styles

Note: answers can be in any order as long as they are under the correct heading.

Hard factors can be easily quantified, while soft factors are more intangible.

160 D

'Style' refers to the style of leadership adopted by the organisation – in this case, an authoritarian approach.

161 B, C, E

Social factors relate to interactions with others. A is a 'job factor', while D is a 'personal' factor. The remaining three options are social factors.

162 A

This resistance appears to have been caused by the employees misunderstanding the rationale behind the cost savings, as QQS has yet to fully explain this to them. Parochial self-interest refers to employees only considering their own needs, rather than that of the business. However, that does not best describe what is described in the scenario as employees do not accurately understand what effect the new system will actually have on them.

163 A

The company is currently in the 'unfreeze' stage, where management is attempting to explain the need for change in an attempt to maximise buy-in by employees and reduce the amount of resistance. Note that 'reinforcement' is not one of Lewin's three stages.

ANSWERS TO OBJECTIVE TEST QUESTIONS : SECTION 2

164

Driving		**Restraining**	
C	The Marketing Director	A	The existing product-oriented culture
D	The new mission statement	B	The length of service by staff
G	Loss of market share	E	Staff background in vehicle maintenance
		F	J's competencies with relationship marketing

Note: answers can be in any order as long as they are under the correct heading.

Driving forces are anything that is pushing the change forward (i.e. the shift to relationship marketing and customer focus). The Marketing Director has authority within the company and is likely to be a major driving force. The new mission statement will help to focus staff on the new requirements for customer focus, while the loss of market share is also an indication that the change is vital for XA to adopt.

Unfortunately there will be issues that hold the organisation back from adopting the necessary changes – the existing culture and long-serving staff are likely to mean that XA is at least somewhat stuck in its ways. Staff may also be uncomfortable with the proposed service focus as they are not used to it, most having a background in vehicle maintenance. Finally, J could be a restraining force herself. She lacks knowledge of relationship marketing and may therefore struggle to implement it.

165 C, D

Refreezing refers to ensuring that employees do not slip back into old ways of working. C and D will help to accomplish this. A and B are both activities within the 'change' stage of the three-stage model, as they are both part of implementing the new system.

166 B

Theory O suggests that an organisation should look to enhance its culture and staff skills. A, C and D would all be examples of this. Theory E involves focus on shareholder value, which usually leads to redundancies, cost reductions and downsizing in a crisis.

167 C

A is unlikely to be successful as staff are already very well rewarded. Offering more is unlikely to motivate them. Training would not deal with the root cause of resistance – the feeling that the business doesn't trust its staff. Also – it is difficult to see that staff members would be willing to take time away from their work to undertake a training course! HO management simply forcing the change through (option D) is also likely to be a failure as HO staff may simply leave, which would be a disaster for the bank as they are a core competence. The only suitable option is to explain the reason for the changes being made – and that it will benefit the organisation (and by extension the employees) as it will prevent HO being prosecuted and heavily fined – which could impact on employee pay and bonuses.

SUBJECT E3 : STRATEGIC MANAGEMENT

168 A, C, D

While the new CEO's change process may involve redundancies or new Board members, it is not a specific requirement of a change leader to undertake these activities.

169 D

G achieved some interim goals, indicating that she generated some short-term wins. She had ensured that senior management agreed to help her implement the vision (i.e. she has created a guiding coalition) as well as informing all staff of her plans (communicating her vision). However, she failed to convince staff of the need for change (establishing a sense of urgency) as they still felt that the company was performing well enough with its existing operations.

170 A, C

Teams can take longer to arrive at a decision, and end up with a compromise position that fails to take account of the needs of the business. However, it should improve the communication between different departments as they will all have representation on the team. In addition, it should improve the review of the team's suggestion as the final decision will have had the input and oversight of a number of different people.

171 B

The other styles are: participation, education and communication, facilitation and support, manipulation and co-optation and negotiation.

172 A2, B4, C3, D1

Remember that manipulation and co-optation involves deliberately distorting the truth to make employees believe that the change is needed.

173 D

G needs to maintain good future relations with its skilled staff members. This tends to rule out manipulation or coercion as options. Negotiation is unlikely to be successful as G is proposing the minimum number of redundancies to avoid insolvency. Education would maintain G's relationship with staff and hopefully help them understand the urgent need for change. As the workforce is small and the redundancies need to be made over a long period, there should be time for G to undertake this approach.

174 B, C, D, E

The change agent can fulfil a wide range of roles within the organisation. However, the ultimate decision about which strategy to adopt will likely be taken by the directors of BB. The change agent will be there to help them make this decision.

175 A, D, E

Options B and C are issues relating to the use of external consultants as change agents. The remaining power skills are: ability to collaborate effectively, ability to develop relationships based on trust, being respectful of the process of change and ability to work across different business functions.

ANSWERS TO OBJECTIVE TEST QUESTIONS : SECTION 2

176

	Executive mentoring		Executive coaching
A	The provider acts as an ongoing role model	C	Is usually undertaken for a specific, defined period
B	Offers wide-ranging, practical advice and support	D	Tends to focus on specific skills and goals
E	More likely to cover both technical and non-technical areas		

Note: answers can be in any order as long as they are under the correct heading.

Remember that mentoring tends to involve the provider acting as a role model and helping and supporting the mentee on an ongoing, as-needed basis. Coaching is often more formal and involves helping the person being coached with specific skills for a defined period.

177 C

This involves HAP repositioning itself in the market in an attempt to once again gain competitive advantage. Retrenchment involves continuing with an existing strategy, but drastically cutting costs.

178 D

Redundancies and reduction in working hours may well be needed if they are to secure P's long-term future. A coercive approach may not make G popular, but there is no ethical requirement to involve staff in the decision making process – particularly if P is in a crisis. However, distorting the facts given to employees would breach G's integrity and is not considered appropriate professional behaviour.

179 B

Successful change leaders recognise, reward and celebrate the accomplishments of their staff, according to Kanter.

180 A, B

Note that D is a feature of Kanter's 'skills for leaders in change-adept organisations' model.

DIGITAL STRATEGY – 15%

DIGITAL TECHNOLOGIES

181 B

The data is changing with great velocity (speed) which may be making it difficult for F to keep his information up to date.

182 B, C, D

Note that the increasing use of electronic devices makes Big Data collection easier. Many organisations successfully gather information from social media sites such as Facebook and Twitter and use it to great effect within their decision-making processes.

183 C

In order for an organisation to properly take advantage of a move to digital, or to survive digital disruption within its industry, the executive leadership team will need to demonstrate a number of abilities.

Inspirational leadership – digitisation will be an exercise in change management, but probably on a bigger and quicker scale than the organisation will typically be used to. **The leadership team will need to energise the workforce and inspire confidence that digitisation is the right way forwards and is being carried out in the right way.**

The move to digital will only succeed if those at the top of the organisation take ownership and persuade others to commit to the change.

184 C

Cloud and mobile computing is computing based on the internet. It avoids the needs for software, applications, servers and services stored on physical computers. Instead it stores these with cloud service providers who store these things on the internet and grant access to authorised users.

185 A

Process automation (also known as Robotic, Digital or Business Process Automation) refers to the use of digital technology to perform a process or processes to accomplish a workflow or function. Or, to put it another way, processes that used to be done manually become automated.

186 A, B, D, E

The Bargaining Power of Suppliers has actually fallen, as they need to engage in greater promotional activity and thus incur significant additional cost.

ANSWERS TO OBJECTIVE TEST QUESTIONS : SECTION 2

187 C

Reinforcement learning is when an algorithm learns to perform a task by trying to maximise the rewards it receives for the actions it takes. For example, in managing an investment fund, the rewards would be gains in value of the fund based on which investments it has decided to put capital into.

Reinforcement learning can be used when there isn't a lot of training data available, the ideal end state cannot be clearly defined, or the only way to learn about the environment is to interact with it.

188 B

Data visualisation is a general term that describes any attempt to take data and help people to understand it better by presenting it in a visual context. Patterns, trends, correlations and other relationships that might otherwise not be noticed in a narrative-type presentation can become clearer and more obvious when presented using some sort of data visualisation software.

189 A, B, D, E

ELEMENTS OF DIGITAL STRATEGY

190 C

Commission – revenue is earned through matching sellers to customers.

191 D

Trading – it is possible to identify circumstances where the demand/supply market forces are producing a sales value which is mispriced. Traders can use technology to identify opportunities to buy at a low price and sell when more realistic prices are in play.

192 B

Build

Building new business models might be the best route when an opportunity is related to the company's core business. The benefits are that it typically maximises control and minimises costs in markets that a company must own because of their strategic importance. If companies decide to go for the build route, they can benefit by creating and developing new products and services.

193 A

Joint venture

A separate business entity whose shares are owned by two or more business entities. Assets are formally integrated and jointly owned.

194 A, B, E

If organisations are to meet these ever-changing needs, it is important that they understand the key drivers behind such change. The following are identified as key factors:

- **Mobile and internet penetration** – the increasing rate of mobile phone ownership, combined with access to the internet (with mobile beginning to exceed broadband). It is reckoned that by 2025 the number of smartphone subscriptions will reach 4 billion, with much of the growth coming from emerging economies.
- **Connected devices** – the number of connected devices are expected to grow from 2.5 billion in 2009 to 30 billion by 2020. This will help enable real-time customisation of products and services.
- **Data analytics and the cloud** – the increasing use of e-commerce platforms, social networks, apps etc will result in increased need for automated data analytics.
- **User interfaces** – advances in how human beings interact with machines (e.g. through voice recognition or motion-tracking systems) means that carrying out tasks becomes quicker and more efficient for humans.
- **Global accessibility** – rising living standards in developing economies means that more and more people are gaining access to the internet and so connectivity.
- **Increasing urbanisation** – the growing percentage of people who live in urban as opposed to rural areas. The United Nations estimates that, from approximately 54% of the global population in 2014, this will grow to almost 60% by 2050.

195 B, D, E

If organisations are to meet these ever-changing needs, it is important that they understand the key drivers behind such change. The following are identified as key factors:

- **Mobile and internet penetration** – the increasing rate of mobile phone ownership, combined with access to the internet (with mobile beginning to exceed broadband). It is reckoned that by 2025 the number of smartphone subscriptions will reach 4 billion, with much of the growth coming from emerging economies.
- **Connected devices** – the number of connected devices are expected to grow from 2.5 billion in 2009 to 30 billion by 2020. This will help enable real-time customisation of products and services.
- **Data analytics and the cloud** – the increasing use of e-commerce platforms, social networks, apps etc will result in increased need for automated data analytics.
- **User interfaces** – advances in how human beings interact with machines (e.g. through voice recognition or motion-tracking systems) means that carrying out tasks becomes quicker and more efficient for humans.
- **Global accessibility** – rising living standards in developing economies means that more and more people are gaining access to the internet and so connectivity.
- **Increasing urbanisation** – the growing percentage of people who live in urban as opposed to rural areas. The United Nations estimates that, from approximately 54% of the global population in 2014, this will grow to almost 60% by 2050.

In essence, more and more people are becoming connected to technology, enjoying the benefits that it delivers, and demanding that such benefits increase, not just within 1 industry but across industries – there is no reason to believe that advances in 1 area of business cannot be transferred to other areas.

'Peer review' and 'Self-service' are changing customer needs, not drivers of that change.

ANSWERS TO OBJECTIVE TEST QUESTIONS : **SECTION 2**

196 A

Design thinking – instead of designing a single product or service that can be marketed to many customers, there should be a shift in mindset to designing many experiences for one customer. This must be mixed with the ability to constantly learn and adapt as customer needs change.

197 A3, B2, C1

Digital traction is a combination of metrics in 3 areas: Scale, Active Usage, and Engagement.

- **Scale** – this relates to the number of people who are showing an interest in the product or service. Typical metrics could include the number of visitors; unique users; the number of registered users; growth in registrations per month; or organic user acquisition.

- **Active usage** – this refers to the frequency with which a user interacts with the organisation. Appropriate metrics could include the number of active users; daily active users (DAU); monthly active users (MAU); conversion rate; abandon rates; the number of repeat users/customers.

- **Engagement** – these measures look at the degree to which the user has engaged with the organisation. Suitable metrics may include time spent on site; Net Promoter Score (NPS); customer satisfaction index; posts contributed; number of likes and shares; photos/videos shared/uploaded and views completed.

198 B, C, D

The CAC is actually $32m/0.09m (it relates to only the increase in registrations), so about $356 per new registered user.

The LTV:CAC ratio is actually about 1.7 times. Calculated as (60 months × $10 per month)/$356 CAC.

199 A, D, E

Engagement – these measures look at the degree to which the user has engaged with the organisation. Suitable metrics may include time spent on site; Net Promoter Score (NPS); customer satisfaction index; posts contributed; number of likes and shares; photos/videos shared/uploaded and views completed.

The number of business angels visiting is a 'scale' metric.

The percentage of business angels who make a second (or subsequent) deal is a measure of 'repeat business', so is an 'active usage' metric.

200 A, C, D

The World Economic Forum proposes the following:

- Formulate a long-term working strategy for millenials – identify the relevant positions that employees will occupy during their career with the company and then create suitable promotional opportunities.

- Work with staff to formulate company values together – this means listening to, and taking note of, the aspirations of those working for the business. Senior management should do this in person, not just as a communication sent company-wide.

- Empower the workforce – and give them incentives to perform e.g. via long term company share plans, project leadership responsibilities or training opportunities.

- Build workspaces that attract digital talent – this relates to the physical layout and appearance of the working environment. Flexibility and a dynamic appearance in the workplace inspires creativity and collaboration. Thought should also be given to allowing staff to work from home on occasions and flexible working hours. should do this in person, not just as a communication sent company-wide.

- Create policies that support collaboration and knowledge-sharing tools – this can include encouraging staff to use platforms such as Facebook@work, Yammer or Sprinklr, or hardware preferences such as being to use your own laptop in the workplace.

201 B

The consultancy group Accenture wrote a report, in 2015, called "Accenture Technology Vision". This report highlighted 5 emerging trends, which were shaping the digital landscape for organisations, on which business leaders should focus when developing digital strategies:

1. **The Internet of Me** – users are being placed at the centre of digital experiences through apps and services being personalised.

2. **Outcome economy** – organisations have an increased ability to measure the outcomes of the services that they deliver; customers are more attracted to outcomes than just simply to products, and this is what organisations should focus on.

3. **The Platform (r)evolution** – global platforms are becoming easier to establish and cheaper to run. Developments such as cloud computing and mobile technology offer huge potential for innovation and quicker delivery of next-generation services. The rate of evolution is only going to increase.

4. **The intelligent enterprise** – using data in a smart way enables organisations to become more innovative and achieve higher degrees of operating efficiency.

5. **Workforce reimagined** – whilst greater use is made of smart machines, the role of human beings is not being removed altogether; they are simply being used in a different way. Ways need to be identified in which man and machines can work effectively together to create better outcomes.